Rebuild Your Tattered Temple

Small Beginnings Toward Better Health

Carol Peterson

Honor Bound Books

Honor Bound Books

Interior graphic Ornament 1 used with permission from Adobe. Typeset in 18/24 Papyrus, 14 pt Viner Hand and 12/16 pt Cambria, used with permission from Microsoft.

Cover by Musa Adam perfect_designx.

ISBN: 9780997778526

Dedication

This book is dedicated to the women in our Lit 'n Lunch book club who worked with me on the very first draft of this book nearly a dozen years ago, sharing the struggles they were facing. Thanks, girlfriends!

Rebuild Your Tattered Temple

Small Beginnings Toward Better Health

Contents

PART V WHAT ELSE GOES IN THE TEMPLE?

PART VI MISCELLANEOUS

Chapter 1

The Temple is Crumbling!

Don't you know that you yourselves are God's temple and that God's Spirit lives in you? (1 Corinthians 3:16).

God created a glorifying temple when He made this body. But over the years, I've turned it into a ramshackle tent that leaks.

Every time I begin again to live a healthier lifestyle, committing to finally conquering my food and exercise issues, the voices begin. You know the ones,

- You'll never succeed.

- You've failed every time before. Why do you think you can do it this time?

- You can't. You won't. You aren't.

Those voices are not of God. God's voice can be clearly heard in Scripture in words of encouragement, hope, and inspiration.

The Temple is Crumbling

Scripture has a lot to say about the health of our physical bodies and also about the connection between our physical health and our spiritual health. We know through Scripture that God wants the best for all of us in all areas of our lives. He wants us to live life abundantly. Part of that means having abundant health, to the best we can have it. Part of the character of God is that He wants to encourage us to keep moving forward. Another part of His character is that He looks at our attempts with love rather than focusing on our past failures.

I began writing this book over ten years ago. The nagging question through it all remained: How can I write a book about regaining health as I watch my own health deteriorate over time?

- You'll never succeed.

- You've failed every time before. Why do you think you can do it this time?

- You can't. You won't. You aren't.

Despite past failures, I have continued to find encouragement in Scripture. I have been reminded that, yes, this body is the temple of the Holy Spirit. What is ultimately more important than my physical health though is my spiritual health—that my heart is clean; my thoughts are pure; my mind is clear. And that understanding comes with the reminder that God has chosen to already see me that way because of His grace.

The Apostle Paul learned a lesson about grace when he asked God to remove a thorn from his side.

> *Three times I pleaded with the Lord to take it away from me. But he said to me, "My grace is sufficient for you, for my power is made perfect in weakness"* (2 Corinthians 12:8-9).

The Temple is Crumbling

Paul asked God to remove a thorn from his side. Whether or not it was a physical thorn, an emotional thorn or spiritual one, God responded "My grace is sufficient for you."

How does that verse relate to a journey towards physical health?

Personally, it caused me to consider the possibility that my struggle with weight is a thorn. Perhaps God is teaching me something about my desire for physical beauty or my relationship with food or Him. Perhaps, it is a way God is keeping me humble. Or perhaps my battle with weight is part of a larger spiritual battle going on around me.

Whatever the reason for my struggle, the truth that the Apostle Paul declared remains: God's grace is sufficient.

- If I fail every time I try, God's grace rests on me.

- God loves me. He has brought me into His family. He has cleansed my soul. He has forgiven my sins. He has promised me eternity with Him through His grace.

- Whatever else happens in this earthly life, I am covered by God's grace. It's all I need, truly.

It's all you need, too.

I have not given up on this body the Holy Spirit and I inhabit. Yes, it is tattered. It is overweight, under exercised, tired, and sluggish. I have not given up however, on attaining and maintaining the best health I am able, with the strength and understanding I have and the strength and understanding Jesus gives me daily.

This book is not a "how to" or even an "I plan to" or an "I wish I could" book. It is not a book spouting specific medical or health advice. I am not an expert on either.

Rather, this is a book about promises from God and verses of Scripture that can encourage us for every part of maintaining or seeking better health—whatever that may mean to you individually and at whatever level of health you have now.

The central inspiration for our rebuilding efforts comes from Zechariah 4:10 (the New Living Translation NLT). When the Jews returned from exile in Babylon, they began rebuilding the temple of the Lord in Jerusalem. They struggled with the enormity of the task, with obtaining building materials, and with local officials who hoped to thwart their work. God's encouragement to His people through Zechariah was this:

> *Do not despise these small beginnings, for the LORD rejoices to see the work begin.*

- We struggle with the work needed to increase or maintain our health.

  But the Lord rejoices to see the work begin.

- We struggle with food choices, exercise programs, and medications we are required to use as building materials.

  But the Lord rejoices to see the work begin.

- We struggle with family and friends who tempt us away from what we need to do or with our inner voice saying, just one piece of cake.

  But the Lord rejoices to see the work begin.

- We are tempted to listen to the evil one who tells us we are not worth the effort.

  But the Lord rejoices to see the work begin.

These bodies don't belong to us. They are the Lord's and we are merely stewards of them for a time. We may never have the health and vitality we had 30 years ago. But we can make small beginnings, knowing the Lord is rejoicing to see the work begin.

Something else happens when we make small beginnings. Doing so and not feeling overwhelmed because they are small, sometimes encourages us to seek to make small beginnings in other areas of our health too. And then in another area of health. Perhaps each of them is a small beginning in themselves, but several small beginnings can add up to an overall improvement greater than when we began.

Each woman faces unique health issues. Some are recovering from a health crisis—a heart attack, stroke, injury, surgery, cancer. Many women struggle with hormonal changes that go from raging to sagging and then leave altogether.

It is each of our responsibilities to understand *our* personal health issues. If you are overeating because of a hormonal imbalance, chemical imbalance, thyroid or psychological problem, you need to address that medically. This book is not about providing health advice. It is about encouraging you to work toward a healthy lifestyle *in addition* to other medical care you need.

Likewise, if you are recovering from a serious health threat or heading toward one, you need to first make sure you address that threat. This book is not about providing health advice. It is about encouraging you to work toward a healthy lifestyle *in addition* to other medical care you need.

Whatever we are facing, the walls of our temple may have begun to sag and crumble. We need shoring up or rebuilding. The last three books of the Old Testament relate how the Jews returned to Jerusalem and began the rebuilding of the temple of God in preparation for the Messiah's coming 500 years later. Did you catch that? Three books of our Holy Bible deal with rebuilding the Temple of the Lord.

Let's look at what the Lord had to say to the Jews through Haggai about rebuilding the Temple of God.

> *"Is it a time for you yourselves to be living in your paneled houses, while this house remains a ruin?"* (Haggai 1:4)

We can smear makeup on our faces to give us a healthy glow, spritz our curls so we appear to bounce with vitality, and become style gurus, so we are the visual epitome of youth. But underneath all that paneling, our health may lie in ruins.

God has given us a gift of our one and only earthly life. And He has given us these bodies to live those lives in. They may not be the bodies we wish we had, nor the heavenly bodies we will receive in Glory, but they are the ones we have now. We can make them the best bodies they can be by doing what God has in mind for us.

We don't start from scratch. God already "began a good work in us." This is about starting where we are, creating a blueprint, gathering our building materials, and learning some construction skills, both for our spiritual growth and our physical rebuilding. Every focus point though begins with Scripture—what it says, what it means, how we can apply it, how it can encourage us.

I have made small beginnings in rebuilding my own tattered temple. I know the Lord is rejoicing along with me. Moreover, I have been blessed by the promises and encouragements in Scripture which remind me that I am a work in progress and that Jesus loves me the way I am right now as well as the woman He is helping me become.

I am praying you, too, will be encouraged.

THINKING IT THROUGH: What voices do you hear when you think about improving your health? Which of the verses of Scripture in this chapter make you feel encouraged about what God wants for your health? How might focusing on that Scripture help you block out other voices meant to discourage you?

PRAYER: Heavenly Father, thank you for the miracle you made when you made me. Thank you, Jesus for becoming human so you could understand my human frailty and for dying on the cross so the Holy Spirit could live in me. Thank you, Holy Spirit for being ever present in me. Please guide and direct me today, as I set out to rebuild your temple by eating, moving, and living in a way that will glorify you. Amen.

SMALL BEGINNINGS
Take an honest inventory of your health. What health problems are you aware of? Make a list of no more than three areas of health you want to address first.

Part I

My Attitude

Chapter 2

I Surrender

For what I do is not the good I want to do; no, the evil I do not want to do—this I keep on doing (Romans 7:19).

Again, and again, God gives us examples in Scripture of people like the Apostle Paul, who struggle just like we do; imperfect folks who love Jesus. These verses encourage us by making us feel that if they can keep trying, we can, too.

How do we "surrender all" when it comes to health? Can you just throw up your hands, say "I give up trying to do it on my own; Jesus I surrender my health to you!" If you are that kind of gal, then good going!

Some of us though, have so many different areas of our health we need to address or habits we need to change, it's almost impossible to remember everything you're supposed to do, much less make new habits. "Surrendering all" may mean first **committing ourselves to follow Jesus** and then surrendering the "doing" a little at a time—attempting small improvements and making those improvements part of our lives until they become natural. Then making another small improvement. Then another.

We are thus "surrendering all" in the sense that we want to do God's will in our lives as it relates to our health. We are surrendering the whole, low-fat-turkey-on-whole-wheat-tortilla enchilada. But then we are chopping the enchilada up into bite-size pieces and surrendering them one at a time, so they become part of our inner being.

Looked at from a spiritual perspective, we're letting the Holy Spirit take us through a refining process. Refining is done in stages, removing first the large impurities and then starting over a second time to remove the next largest impurities; then the next.

I am reminded of Philippians 1:6

> *"...being confident of this, that he who began a good work in you will carry it on to completion until the day of Christ Jesus."*

This verse doesn't say God took over and completed all changes the instant we came to Him. Rather it says that God began to work, and that work will continue on until He is done. The very physical surrendering we're speaking of in this chapter—surrendering what we need to do for good health—first involves our spiritual surrender to God's will.

Would Jesus love it if I surrendered everything about my health right now? All at once? If I never let another grain of white sugar pass my lips? If I got up every morning, ran 5 miles, did 50 pushups, and drank gallons of pure, crystal water? Sure, He'd love it.

I Surrender

But would He be happy if I surrendered everything over time? If I started by becoming aware of what I need to do and began making those changes today, making more changes tomorrow, and more the day after that?

My guess is that He would love that, too.

In fact, our focus Scripture from Zechariah reminds us of that truth.

> *Do not despise these small beginnings for the LORD rejoices to see the work begin* (Zechariah 4:10 NLT).

We can think of surrendering our unhealthy habits in the same way. If we're not able to surrender every bad habit right now, can we surrender all of it, piece by piece over time, with the understanding that God, through our faith in Jesus and through the workings of the Holy Spirit, will help us do what we need to do? It is surrendering all. A little now; more later.

Each of us has health issues we need to surrender. God is going to have His way with us regardless of what we do. But we can stop hindering Him. We can make what He wants to do easier both for Him and for us. Not everyone needs to lose weight. Not everyone struggles to get adequate exercise or to drink enough water. Not everyone is going through or recovering from a health crisis. But we can all use improvement. We can all use encouragement. Most especially, we all have room to grow our faith in Christ. Remember Proverbs 16:9.

> *In his heart a man plans his course, but the Lord determines his steps.*

In our hearts we can plan our course. We can decide to improve our health. We can determine what areas of health we need to improve and prioritize them. Then we can ask the Lord to determine those steps. We can surrender all.

One habit or change at a time.

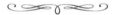

THINKING IT THROUGH: What three areas of your health do you need to surrender to God? Write them down. We are now in the preparation stage for change. The next step is action. The final stage is maintenance of the changes we have made. Just like surrender, we will take each stage one at a time. A little now; more later.

PRAYER: Heavenly Father, thank you for making my purpose so simple—to obey you. Forgive me when I try to make my purpose more complicated. Remind me to simply obey you in all things. Holy Spirit help me to be obedient today. Then, Jesus, change my heart so that your desires are mine. Amen.

SMALL BEGINNINGS
What three areas of your health do you need to surrender to God? What small beginning can you take today in surrender?

Chapter 3

Stop Thwarting God's Miracle

For you created my inmost being; you knit me together in my mother's womb. I praise you because I am fearfully and wonderfully made; your works are wonderful, I know that full well (Psalm 139:13-14).

Think back to fifth grade science. Come on, you can do it! You sat next to Teddy Williams, remember? Back when he was cute. Yeah, now you're there.

In fifth grade, we learned that the cells in our bodies are continuously dying and new cells are being created to replace the old ones. In other words, parts of our bodies are made completely new every minute. Parts of our bodies are made completely new every day. And...are you ready for this revelation? It also means we are a completely new person, through and through—from our you'll-never-guess-my-real-color hair to our overly-fluffy-portable-pillowed bottoms—every few years, accomplished as part of the on-going miracle God created.

If we're continuously being made completely new, there is hope. Hope, because our rebuilding is a process that has already begun without us doing a thing. Also, we have hope because the rebuilding process doesn't stop until we stop permanently.

Hope, because it's never too late to jump in and help the process.

Not only can I be made new spiritually when I renew my dedication and my relationship to Christ; not only can I be renewed psychologically every day when I renew my determination to do healthy things. It also means that I am *literally* made new throughout my lifetime, top to bottom, inside and out—one cell at a time.

God has created this body to renew itself on its own. That takes a load off my worry that "I have to rebuild this temple by myself."

Think of a construction project. In our *re*-construction, God, the Father is the general contractor. He has the plan, the blueprint, and the vision of what we are meant to be.

Christ is the foundation of the whole project; the city building manager.

The Holy Spirit is the project superintendent. He guides and counsels us to remind us what we should be doing.

All I am in this project is the laborer. I'm not in charge. I may have my own ideas, but it would be better if I just follow God's plan.

Can you imagine a construction project where everybody had their own set of blueprints but none of the blueprints were the same?

Some of us have been following our own plan hastily sketched on a used napkin. The ink is blurred and there's a suspicious greasy spot in the center. Not surprisingly, our temples have started to fall apart. It's time to crumple our plan into a ball, toss it as far as we can (to get some exercise) and pull out God's blueprint instead. God's plan is perfect. Perfection is always a good plan to follow.

Hope is the full assurance of what can be done. In this case our hope is even more solid because we know the change is already happening. God created a plan that doesn't require us to do anything, yet our bodies will be partially rebuilt on their own.

Our responsibility is to not do anything to inhibit those good changes from happening.

If we create extra fatty, lazy, blobby cells that our bodies have to spend extra time fixing; if we don't drink pure, cleansing water to flush out our cells; if we don't move to lubricate our joints and flex tendons, then God's perfect plan gets gummed up *by us*.

Simply focusing on living healthy *today*, on the other hand, helps ensure a more healthful tomorrow. We just have to let the ongoing rebuilding process work as God created it. In other words, if we do what we should do today, then our beautiful temples *have already been rebuilt in the future* because they *are* being rebuilt right now as old cells die and new ones are created.

Think of it as a time warp. We know it will happen because we're doing the right things now which will change what we become tomorrow. Today we rebuild our temple from the outside in (what we do) while God rebuilds it from the inside out. It can happen in the future (or not) based on what we do today.

In the same way, we can hope in Christ spiritually. If we profess Christ as our savior, then we know we will be saved eternally because we already are saved based on what Jesus already did—when He declared "It is finished" before dying on the cross.

In other words, our spiritual future is set because of what Jesus already did.

God *is doing* a good work in us and in our health because He already began it. We can help the process by what we do or do not do today.

Think of your body as a car. Pick your favorite. Mine is a Jaguar XJ12. It's black with lots of shiny chrome, cushy leather seats, and that gorgeous leaping jaguar on the hood.

I bring my Jaguar home from the dealership and everything works like it should. It's powerful, smooth riding, and beautiful. But then I run out of gas. Instead of using a high grade of gasoline I put in whatever I have handy in my pantry. Here's a brown liquid. Molasses. With molasses in the tank, that beautiful car isn't going to run perfectly. In fact, it won't run at all.

Or I decide to sit in my beautiful Jaguar with the engine running so I can listen to the stereo system, leave the air conditioner running, and the lights on while I do. Mighty comfortable and pleasant. Until everything stops. That beautiful car isn't going to run perfectly with a dead battery. In fact, it won't run at all.

Or, I want to make sure my beautiful Jaguar stays beautiful. So, I park it in the garage, cover it up with a sheet, and never even start the engine. Even if I don't turn the car on, the battery will still be dead, and that beautiful car won't run perfectly. In fact, it won't run at all.

To keep the car operating, I must give it gasoline, not overuse it but make sure I get it out and running. That's the minimum. If I want to keep the car working *well*, I have to take it out on the highway from time to time to get those RPMs up and revving. I have to make sure the tires are inflated properly and are free from holes. I have to feed it good quality, clean oil regularly and change the filters. I also have to watch brake fluid levels, replace the wipers, and take care of all the little details that contribute to the smooth running of my car. And if I want it to be beautiful, I have to wash it and polish it until it gleams. I have to take care of my machine.

My body machine, too.

God gave me a wonderful body—powerful and beautiful. But I eat low quality food, stay up too late, and run myself ragged. Why do I expect it to run as well as it would if I took good care of it by giving it good quality food, moving it regularly and enough, and getting adequate rest?

God created our bodies to work on their own. We breathe in and out without having to tell ourselves to. Our hearts pump blood into our toes and through our brains without us having to direct it. Even our spleens do whatever spleens do without us wagging our fingers at them.

We're a machine that God has placed on autopilot. But even on autopilot, we still have to watch traffic, check the speedometer, and turn the wheel so we stay on the road. We have to do the same with our bodies. It's called "our responsibility." What does that leave for us to do?

Two things.

I Have to Stop Messing Up God's Miracle

The first thing we have to do is the one many of us struggle with the most. We have to let the miracle work by not doing the things that prevent it from being the best miracle it can be. Like what we eat, taking in harmful substances, doing what is not healthy—things that cause God's miracle to sputter and fitz. Need a biblical example?

The parting of the Red Sea was one of God's coolest miracles. The Israelites escaping from Egypt; Pharaohs' troops racing after them. God parts the waters. The Israelites walk right through the Sea, cross to the other side, and then God closes the waters and washes the Egyptian army away. Gotta love a simple plan like that.

Fortunately, the Israelites understood God's miracle and went with the flow. They walked through the path God created for them. But what if God did His awesome miracle—parted the Red Sea and then Moses said, "Hey, I think there's a bridge up the road. Let's go that way instead."

If the Israelites hadn't crossed the Red Sea through the path of God's miracle but had taken a different route instead, the Egyptian army might have caught up with them and we would have a very different version of the Old Testament. Instead, they recognized the miracle God created and didn't try to think up a better idea on their own.

With our bodies, God made a great miracle. We need to *not* do things to mess it up. Like smoking or using harmful or addictive substances.

This part of our responsibility is not about doing anything. It's about *not doing* anything stupid. God is calling us to *inaction*? Yep. When you think about it that way, it should be easy to just not do things. It's all about letting the miracle work by not doing bad stuff; like not poisoning our bodies with unhealthy substances.

I Have to Do My Part

The second thing about letting the miracle work *is* about doing our part to improve on what God has given us. When God parted the Red Sea, the Israelites could have said, "Wow, will you look at that! It's a miracle!" Then they could have sat on the beach, pulled out their picnic lunches of grilled lamb on unleavened bread and sang, "Down by the Riverside." Sure, that's an example of not doing things to gum up God's miracle. But it wouldn't have gotten them very far from Pharaoh either.

Instead, the Israelites recognized the miracle and crossed the Red Sea. They used the miracle as God intended, *doing* what he intended them to.

God made the miracle of our bodies. That was His part. He intends us to not gum them up. He also expects us to do our part to make the miracle all it can be. So, this second part of taking care of God's miracle bodies is that we do what we can so that these machines purr and rev like God intended.

We're to eat God's perfect miracle food, move in ways and amounts that God intended us, and get the sleep, love, friendship, prayer, and other things we need.

Sometimes we feel discouraged while we're trying to rebuild our temple. We cry out. "I'm in such a mess. I need a miracle!" We have to remember: God has already given us the miracle. We need to let the miracle body He created work as He planned.

It's the same with the miracle of salvation. There's no way we could ever earn our salvation. So, God created a way for Himself to be the miracle. He gave Himself—Jesus—as the only sacrifice acceptable to Himself when He sacrificed Himself *to* Himself. God gives us grace and mercy to cover the things we've done to gum up our spiritual selves. He now expects us to draw near to Him, follow the Spirit's leading, and do the things that will allow Him to continue to work in our hearts until Jesus' return.

God is in the business of miracles. He made a big miracle when He created us. Recognition of that miracle is the first step to working to keep the miracle going.

THINKING IT THROUGH: This understanding that God created our bodies as living, breathing, *ongoing* miracles is something big. The intricacies involved in this ongoing miracle are staggering.

One of the first steps in successfully reaching your goal is in having a full assurance that it can be achieved. Spend time today thinking about what is going on in your body without you having to do anything about it. Reflect on the promise in Scripture that God *began* a good work (a miracle) in us—not only in body but in spirit. Praise God for His miraculous work in your life and in the lives of those you love.

PRAYER: Heavenly Father, help me recognize that I am a miracle. Help me see that you created my body to work on its own but that I have to stop undermining your miracle and do my part to let your miracle work as you designed. Amen.

SMALL BEGINNINGS
What are you doing to prevent the miracle of your body from functioning perfectly? What do you need to stop doing? What do you need to start doing? What first steps can you take?

Part II

Food

Chapter 4

Starting the Day with Jesus

In the morning, O LORD, you hear my voice; in the morning I lay my requests before you and wait in expectation (Psalm 5:3).

Sleep provides us with a break from the reality of the world we live in. Emotionally and spiritually, morning provides us with an opportunity to begin again. To recommit. To try harder.

As it relates to our rebuilding project, if we failed to follow our plan yesterday, if we fell back into unhealthy habits, we have another chance today to do it right. And the best way to get started toward successfully being obedient is to begin our day with God. To attune our desires to God's. To ask the Holy Spirit to help us live today for Jesus.

When we start our day without God, we start our day alone. We think, "What shall I do today?" Our mind races about, flitting from idea to idea, from one must-do to another. We create mental lists so we can remember our must-do's long enough to write them down on paper. Or we keep paper and pencil by our beds so those first must-do's are firmly settled.

Starting the Day with Jesus

We, me, I, my. That's how we start our day if we start it without God.

But if we start our day with God, we ask, "What do you have in store for me today, God? What is your desire for my heart and for my life? Where will you lead me? How will you show me your love today? Who will you place in my life today that you want me to love on your behalf?"

Our days don't always go as we plan. Some days are glorious; filled with soft sunshine and joyful experiences. We just know God is smiling directly on *me*. Other days are filled with troubles, mistakes, setbacks or pain. And some days just move time forward, clicking minutes of the clock until the day is over and we crawl back into bed, hoping tomorrow will be brighter.

But even if your day is ho-hum or troubled, there's one thing that remains constant. If you start your day with God, you are assured that He's walking with you every step. He is anyway but starting your day with Him *reminds* you of that fact. It alerts you to His presence and sensitizes you to His Spirit—the Holy Spirit living inside this temple. God makes every day new and continues to provide you with a daily opportunity to start it with Him.

One of my favorite verses in Scripture is John 21:12.

> *Jesus said to them, "Come and have breakfast." None of the disciples dared ask him, "Who are you?" They knew it was the Lord.*

A command for us to eat breakfast? A confirmation that breakfast is indeed the most important meal of the day, just as Mom always said?

Maybe; maybe not.

Definitely though, this verse was an invitation to Jesus' disciples to spend time with Him. As Jesus' modern-day disciples, this verse is also an invitation for us to spend time with Him. Right at the beginning of each new day.

For those of us facing food issues, starting the day both with Jesus and food should definitely make breakfast the most important meal of the day.

When it comes to our rebuilding project, if we had trouble yesterday, today is a day for renewing our commitment and doing what we can do *today*. Every day we fail to make a change is simply a day without change. It doesn't mean you've failed worse than ever.

It only means you failed to make a change yesterday. But every day we *do* follow our plan is one more day we have made a change for the better; one more day in which our new, healthy habits are more solidly a part of our new, healthier lifestyle. God gave us the free will to make decisions and to take action. He also modeled grace and forgiveness.

So, each new day is another day to make small beginnings on rebuilding our temple in a way that makes our Lord rejoice.

Let's look at breakfast in a constructive way to help us plan. We have a myriad of breakfast choices. Some are healthy. Some are not. In fact, some are healthy for us; but not for other people who have different health issues.

For example, a healthy breakfast for a diabetic might be eggs and turkey bacon. But that might be an unhealthy breakfast for a person with high cholesterol. For that person, a healthy breakfast might be oatmeal and fruit, which might send a diabetic's blood sugar levels soaring.

We must each clearly understand our own bodies and what makes them function best. We do that through personal experience coupled with sound medical advice from our doctors.

Then we do our best to follow that sound medical advice—taking small building steps as needed.

On the other hand, maybe it's not what we eat for breakfast that we need to adjust, but when. Some of us simply cannot get ourselves moving (not even our mouths!) first thing in the morning. Personally, I'd rather sleep than eat, which means no way am I willing to get up an extra 15 minutes to allow for breakfast.

Think about your hunger patterns and your schedule. Do you start the day ravenous or does the beast growl in earnest about 10:00 am? Do you typically have an early lunch or a late lunch? If you have a late lunch, might having breakfast at 10:00 make more sense than trying to figure out how to get in an early breakfast and a mid-morning snack before lunch? How can you work within your present schedule to make small beginnings toward better health?

Although we are all created according to God's plan, our bodies are unique. We have different tastes, problem foods, and scheduling issues. There are ways to enable ourselves to do the things we need to do with as little pain and effort as possible. But we have to figure out what works for us and then do it.

That's the way it is spiritually, too. We are all created to need God. And Jesus' sacrifice was for all people, all sins, all time. But we are each unique. We have different theological doctrines that pique us or puzzle us or attributes of God that we praise more than other attributes. Each of us might need to figure out how to individualize our worship of God and how best to go about being obedient to His commands for our own, unique lives.

By His example with his disciples, Jesus told us to come and have breakfast—to spend time with Him.

Eating breakfast isn't God's Eleventh Commandment but this Scripture undeniably implies that breakfast was a part of Jesus' day—even His resurrected day. It was also part of His fellowship with those who loved Him. It can be the same for us.

THINKING THROUGH: Do mornings make you feel like you have another chance to get it right? Can you use the sense of new beginnings to recommit to doing what is important?

How does John speak to you? How can you make your morning time with God uniquely yours?

What does a typical breakfast look like for you? Do you need to change it to a healthier version?

PRAYER: Heavenly Father, thank you for the instructions you give us through scripture. Open my heart as to how you want me to apply that instruction to my life. Thank you for making me teachable. Jesus, thank you for giving me an example for life through your relationship with your disciples and that you invite me to begin each day with you. Amen.

SMALL BEGINNINGS
What can you do to begin your day with Jesus? What do
you need to change in your eating habits as a small step
to begin the day with a focus on better health?

Chapter 5

God Made all Things Good

Daniel resolved not to defile himself with the royal food and wine and he asked the chief official for permission not to defile himself this way (Daniel 1:8).

I know in my heart that God's food is better than what man has created. But processed food is so easy, tastes so good. It is practically irresistible to just open a can, plop it down on a plate, and dig in.

Isn't it interesting that Daniel looked at "royal food" as something that would defile his body? To everybody else, royal food would seem like the very best stuff. Saved for the king. It should have been an honor and an extra special treat to be given a portion of such tasty, delicious food.

But if we think about royal food as if it were ancient junk food, then the idea of it defiling Daniel's body might make a whole lot more sense. Put in terms we can understand, maybe the royal food was fatty cream and high cholesterol meat. Maybe the desserts were little more than piles of nutrient-lacking carbohydrates. Or maybe there was just too much of it, so that Daniel's "portion" was way more than he needed.

Whatever *royal food* referred to, we do know that Scripture tells us it wasn't what God intended for Daniel and his friends to eat. Scripture is filled with commands from God about food. But notice God is always talking about the food *He* created; not the processed stuff we invented. Let's start with Genesis 2:15-17

> *Then God said, "I give you every seed-bearing plant on the face of the whole earth and every tree that has fruit with seed in it. They will be yours for food."*

God originally made us vegetarians. Wow. That's a thinker. He gave us "authority" over the animals and Adam even got to name them. But for eating, all God gave us was seed-bearing plants and fruit—except the fruit from that *one* tree of course!

Ignoring the theology behind the story of Adam and Eve noshing on God's forbidden fruit, just look in terms of their eating pattern. God gave them all that awesome, delicious, nutritious food to eat and did they stop there? Nope. Gotta have the *forbidden* food as well. There's probably a correlation with Scripture we could make about modern foods we desire that should be forbidden in our eating plan. But back to God's plan.

After the flood, God expanded humanity's diet by letting us eat meat. In Genesis 9: 3-4, God told Noah,

> *"Everything that lives and moves will be food for you. Just as I gave you the green plants, I now give you everything."*

So now we can eat meat. Later, God restricted the types of meat we could eat. Read through Deuteronomy 14 on your own for the specific restrictions, which God gave the Israelites back then.

God Made All Things Good

God also gave the Israelites manna to eat in the desert, which was described as food from heaven. Still, God restricted the Israelites' eating of it. They could only eat what was given that one day. If they horded it for tomorrow, it went bad. God's specific dietary guidelines included not just the "what" but the "how much."

Things changed after Jesus arrived. Here's Acts 10:15:

> *The voice spoke to him* (Peter) *a second time, "Do not call anything impure that God has made clean."* (explanation added)

In Acts, God told Peter that everything God made is permissible to be eaten.

Unfortunately, we took God's bounty and ran with it.

First, we ran over to the mill and ground up God's nutritious grain, so it had no fiber left.

Then we ran over to the laundromat and dumped bleach into God's beautiful flour, so it had no nutrients left.

Then we ran over to the pharmacy and dumped manmade vitamins back into the flour so we could call it "food" again.

Then because the flavor was all gone, we ran to the chemical department and dumped in ingredients we can't even pronounce.

The only good thing about what we did is the exercise we got from all that running.

We know intuitively that God's fresh food, grown without pesticides and hormones, is better than what man has done to it. But still it's hard and sometimes expensive to ignore man's food and return to God's.

I sometimes think man had outside encouragement in turning away from God's perfect food. For example,

God created beautiful sugar beets. Then man turned them into white sugar that upsets our perfectly balanced blood chemistry. And Satan watched as man became diabetic and had his limbs amputated so man can no longer be God's hands and feet in the world.

God made nutritious food to fuel our bodies so we could have energy to do His will. And Satan watched man stuff himself with junk food so he didn't have energy to do God's will or do it well.

God made every kind of delicious food so we could live a long life and live it abundantly. And Satan watched man pollute his body until it was diseased and bloated and watched as man died prematurely from heart attacks and strokes.

Satan knows that some of those people who died early might have accepted Christ's gift of salvation if they'd lived an extra year or month or day. The truth is that we don't have forever to accept Christ. And we don't have forever to do His work. For certain, we only have now.

We should therefore make the most of what time we have. **This chapter isn't about what specific food categories to eat or not eat. If you are a vegetarian, don't eat meat. If you're allergic to peanuts God doesn't want you to eat them anyway. This chapter is about determining what works for you and then making sure that within those guidelines, we focus on God's perfect food *more* than man's junk.**

Somewhere in the past 50 years, convenience, packaged, and processed became the norm. And we've become dependent upon that convenience. Not all of us are psychologically ready or time-wise able to switch from fast-food dinners to making everything from scratch. But we can make little changes to begin the process.

The Lord rejoices in small beginnings, remember?

If we're not now eating any fresh fruit or vegetables, we can start by having one fresh fruit or one fresh vegetable a day or slowly moving from canned to frozen to fresh over time.

The Lord rejoices in small beginnings.

If organically grown fruit and vegetables are too expensive for our budget, we can commit to soaking and scrubbing the fresh fruit and vegetables we do buy to make them as clean as possible. Or we can start a garden and plant one or two vegetables we like best.

The Lord rejoices in small beginnings.

If we can't suddenly eat only God's foods, we can first try to just eat *more* of God's food than man's food. We can increase the amount of God's food so eventually we are not eating any of man's food on a regular basis.

If we have outlined a goal for what we believe is the best and healthiest eating plan for us, what small beginnings can we put in place to get there? Will it be less red meat and more fish? More fruits and veggies? Less white sugar and flour? What will we do to move toward being in line with eating God's perfect food?

Here's a final thought to consider. It takes a little longer to prepare fresh God foods than to open a man-made package. But the fewer packages of man's food we consume, perhaps the longer life (and better health) we will have.

In other words, eating man's food may save time *now* only to give us less time on this earth in the future.

Heaven will be wonderful; but most of us still want to cling to as much time here on earth as we can. Like the country song says: everybody wants to go to heaven; but nobody wants to go now." (Written by Jim Collins and Marty Dodson; recorded by Kenney Chesney.)

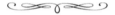

THINKING IT THROUGH: Can you switch from canned fruit and vegetables to frozen and then later to fresh? Or can you prepare three healthy main courses one day, have one for dinner tonight and freeze two for later to help you avoid fast or processed food when you are pressed for time?

Can you commit to having fish one night a week or switch from ground beef to ground turkey? Or half ground beef/half ground turkey first? If you can't afford the higher price of organic fruits and vegetables, can you commit to thoroughly washing the pesticides from the ones you buy? Can you switch from white rice to brown rice? What can you do?

PRAYER: Thank you Heavenly Father for your bounty of perfect food. Forgive me when I desire food made by man more than food made by you. Instill in my heart, Holy Spirit a desire for your perfect food. Instill in my mind the commitment to eat your perfect food. Instill in my mouth a preference for the taste of your perfect food. Use my eating, Jesus, to defeat Satan's desire to prevent me from living my life for you. Amen.

SMALL BEGINNINGS
What one thing can you do today to incorporate more of
God's food into your eating and less of man's junk?

Chapter 6

Bounty Means Variety, Not Volume

Give us today our daily bread (Matthew 6:11).

Theologically, many commentaries claim the phrase "daily bread" means whatever we need to live (emotionally and spiritually as well as physically). As it applies to our study here, "give us this day our daily bread" could simply be a request that God provide us with the food we need to survive this day. It's not a request to give us more food than we need. It's not a request to give us what we need tomorrow. It's a request that God give us what we need today.

In the last chapter we talked about the choices of food we make. If we pray the Lord's Prayer literally, then, we could ask God to "give us today our 100% whole grain bread with plenty of fiber and no trans fats, cholesterol or artificial flavor."

We know we should make nutritious choices in the foods we consume to fuel our bodies. Any good book on nutrition will tell you what amount of servings you need from the various food groups. Certainly, we are what we eat and if we're going to rebuild the temple, we need to build it with quality building blocks—nutritious food made by God.

Remember Noah? When the ark landed on dry land, God told Noah He would never again destroy the world by water. Then He set the rainbow in the sky as a reminder of His promise. You've probably heard the nutritional advice that you should "eat the rainbow." That advice suggests you eat foods that come in every color—from purple cabbage to yellow squash to red peppers to orange oranges.

I like to think of eating the rainbow as fueling our bodies with God's promise. Now that nutritionists are telling us to eat all the colors of food, it's like the medical community is reminding us of God's promise that He intends good health for us and has provided a sign of that promise in the form of a rainbow bounty of food choices for us to enjoy.

This chapter on bounty, however, isn't about food choices. It's about how much we eat. You will notice that Jesus didn't teach us to pray by saying, "give us more food than we need and let us stuff it in our mouths as fast as we can."

Looking at other Scripture, we find support for that last application, when God provided the Jews with the supernatural food, manna while they were in the desert. He only sent enough manna for them to eat each day. No hording it so they could stuff themselves tomorrow.

In fact, Scripture indicates that God does not want us to overeat. Remember the City of Sodom? Sodom was filled with so many evil people that God destroyed the whole city and everyone in it.

> *"Now this was the sin of your sister Sodom: She and her daughters were arrogant, overfed and unconcerned...Therefore I did away with them as you have seen"* (Ezekiel 16:49).

Did you notice that little word jump out of Scripture and flop around the page? One of those reasons God detested the people of Sodom so much? They were "overfed." Uh-oh. Notice also how God specifically refers to the city of Sodom as a female? Without going into a theological discussion, let's just ponder the idea that He was speaking to *us*, girlfriends, and *our* overeating!

Is overeating one of your problems? It's one of mine. I know the tricks. Slow down your eating so your brain has time to tell your stomach it's full. Or is it vice versa? Eat on smaller plates to trick yourself into thinking you're eating more. Understand what an actual portion size is and measure it out before you dump it onto your plate.

The ultimate point though is that the goal of eating is to consume enough but not too much.

Want another Scripture about eating enough but not too much?

Let's go back to the Old Testament when Elisha fed 100 men with only twenty loaves of barley bread.

> *Then he set it before them, and they ate and had some left over, according to the word of the Lord* (2 Kings 5:42-44).

Sound like a familiar theme? Here's Matthew 15:35-38:

> *He* (Jesus) *told the crowd to sit down on the ground. Then he took the seven loaves and the fish, and when he had given thanks, he broke them and gave them to the disciples, and they in turn to the people. They all ate and were satisfied. Afterward the disciples picked up seven basketfuls of broken pieces that were left over. The number of those who ate was four*

thousand, besides women and children" (explanation added).

Jesus fed the crowd enough food, so no one went hungry but still there was food left over. (See also Matthew 14:15-21; Mark 6:31-44; Luke 9:10-17; John 6:5-15)

Again, and again Scripture illustrates God's recognition that we need food to live and be healthy. Jesus came to bring life so that we might live it abundantly. This is meant spiritually, but if we're seeking applications to life, living abundantly as it relates to food isn't about the amount of food God wants us to eat. Neither is bounty. God provided bounty in terms of variety. He gave us that bounty to choose from; not to eat all of it, all the time, in whatever amount we want.

I like the New International Version translation of the abundant life reference. John 10:10 quotes Jesus saying: "I have come that they may have life, and have it to the full." That translation is a clever reminder that when it comes to eating, we are to eat until we are full; not beyond. When Jesus fed thousands of people with a few loaves of bread and a few fish, notice how the passage ended? There were baskets full of bread pieces left but all the people "ate and were satisfied."

We too should strive to eat to be satisfied; not overfed. Otherwise we might end up like the people of Sodom.

THINKING IT THROUGH: Do you need to focus on not eating too much at each meal? Can you measure out portion sizes ahead of time so that you are aware of what you're eating before you find yourself eating more than you need? Can you slow the speed of your eating so that you give your brain time to recognize satisfaction? Can you stop eating mid meal and evaluate your hunger level?

PRAYER: Heavenly Father, thank you for your bounty of healthful, delicious food. Help me, Holy Spirit to eat to fuel my body and listen to it so that I stop eating when I have fueled it satisfactorily. Jesus, thank you for your miraculous examples of feeding the thousands so that all could eat and be satisfied. Amen.

SMALL BEGINNINGS
Do you need to focus on portion control?
What one thing can you do today to help?

Part III

Our Eating Mindset

The following chapters have to do with general reasons for bad eating. If you have a serious concern about eating for psychological reasons, please see a doctor.

Chapter 7

Reasons We Overeat: The Good

Share with God's people who are in need. Practice hospitality (Romans 12:12).

Folks are always telling me I have the spiritual gift of hospitality. Sure, I have lots of people at my house for meetings and dinners but is it a breeze? Nope. Every time, like clockwork, 30 minutes before my guests arrive, I go into "panic mode."

That's why I like this Scripture. It doesn't say: relish in being hospitable; or perfect hospitality or even do hospitality well. It says "practice" hospitality. My personal interpretation and application: Hospitality will never be easy or stress-free. So, just keep practicing.

And what does that have to do with health? I think it means it's our job not only to feed ourselves healthy, nutritious foods but to expand that duty when we feed others. I used to think I should feed my guests comfort foods to make them feel loved. You know the ooey, gooey stuff, piled with calories, fat, and carbs.

Nobody should *ever* eat it but for some reason we conclude it's okay for special occasions; even preferred. Now I'm thinking the best way to show someone you love them is to feed their bodies high-quality fuel that will help them live better and longer.

While I was writing this book, a friend was beginning chemotherapy. This sweet gal had a young family. As I was praying for her the day before she was to start therapy, the Holy Spirit simply said, "Carol, feed my sheep."

I recognize that when Christ originally said those words he was speaking about spiritual feeding. But this time, I knew also that the Holy Spirit was personally telling me to *literally* feed Lisa's family so she would have one less thing to worry about while she was recovering from treatment.

I began my day the next morning in prayer for Lisa. And again, the Holy Spirit said, "Carol, feed my sheep." I responded, "Thank you for the reminder, Holy Spirit. I will cook up a casserole for Lisa's family today."

I went to the grocery store to buy ingredients for a casserole and once again I heard, "Carol, feed my sheep." I felt happy to think I was hearing and following (sometimes a rarity) the instructions of the Holy Spirit. I picked up a package of chicken for the planned casserole and thought to myself, *I'll make a double recipe and freeze a casserole, so I won't have to cook one night in the future.*

'Ain't I clever?

In the process of cooking, I experienced a loaves-and-fishes miracle because my planned 2-casserole cooking event produced one casserole for Lisa and four casseroles for the freezer. After I cleaned up the kitchen, I sat down to read my emails. There in my inbox was an email from another friend who had learned she had cancer and was going to start radiation therapy within the next few weeks.

Once again, I heard the Holy Spirit. "Carol, feed my sheep." Then I understood. Sheep is plural. God was telling me He wanted me to minister to others by literally feeding them—providing whoever He placed in my path with meals to lessen their burdens in a tangible way.

Providing meals for others has always appealed to me on an intellectual level, much the same way that I think it's a terrific idea to donate a kidney. But I'm not overly fond of cooking for my own family. Cooking for someone else is almost too much to consider.

Then I recognized that the Holy Spirit had prepared me to feed flocks of sheep by showing me that I could make several dinners at once, whenever I had the time to do it. Then when there was a need, I could leap at the opportunity to do something practical.

What I learned through that experience is that hospitality doesn't just refer to people who come into your home. It extends beyond the walls of your house and into other peoples' homes. God began to work in my heart.

First, God showed me it could be easy to be generous by cooking when it was convenient. Then something else happened. The Holy Spirit nudged me to understand that as long as I was making meals anyway, they might as well be healthy—especially for people who are going through a health crisis.

Interestingly when I looked up the meaning of hospitality, one dictionary referred me to the related word "hospital." The archaic meaning for hospital is a charitable home, hospice, or school. That takes us to thinking of our home as a place of healing as well as charity and graciousness. And taken literally, if you're not providing healthy food when you're practicing hospitality, your guests could end up in the hospital!

Hospitality may not always happen inside a home. We've all gone to a restaurant to celebrate a birthday; to a wedding to celebrate the beginning of a shared life; to a family reunion to celebrate lives well lived. Whatever the occasion, there's always food. Usually lots of it. Those occasions are very good reasons celebrate. But those very good reasons to celebrate are very bad reasons for bad eating. So, what can we do?

We can focus on the reason for the celebration instead of the substance we are celebrating with. In other words, we can focus on giving and receiving the love that is the center of the occasion. We can focus on being with people we care about. We can focus on the joy of the event. We can let the food just be there like the napkins and the tables and the china and let the celebration be the focus.

In fact, we can celebrate in a way that the Lord can rejoice in small beginnings by keeping in mind our reasons for eating.

Bad eating for good reasons can also be a problem on the receiving end of hospitality. How do you react when someone wants to show you love by feeding *you* comfort food? Do you say to yourself, "Hurray! I *must* eat all this food right now to make sure my hostess knows I feel loved!"

Or do you staunchly resist the food, telling your hostess that you're on a diet and must not touch it—only to watch your hostess's face slide into the top of that delicious chocolate mousse? How gracious would that be?

Once again, we can focus on the reason for the food; not the food itself. We can recognize that our hostess is trying to show us love.

We can express our sincere gratitude for her time and effort and most especially for the love behind it.

Then we can take a small amount of the love offering. We can focus whole heartedly on the social aspects of the hospitality—loving and being loved. We can eat some of the food. Savor it and express our appreciation for it. We can "feed" our hostess's need to know that what she has done to love us is recognized and appreciated. We can focus on the love, rather than on the food itself.

In all things, God wants us to focus on the love—on His love for us; on our love for Him; and on loving others in His name. Jesus told us:

> *"Love the Lord your God with all your heart and with all your soul and with all your mind and with all your strength. The second is this: 'Love your neighbor as yourself.' There is no commandment greater than these"* (Mark 12:31).

As we strive to love God by showing our love to others, we can keep in mind the area of food as a way to love others as we love ourselves. We can feed ourselves and others healthy, nutritious foods in amounts that show our love by nourishing our bodies so that we may love God and others longer, better, and with more energy. We can keep Proverbs 11:25 in mind.

> *Those who refresh others will themselves be refreshed.*

Sometimes in life we find ourselves eating bad for good reasons. It has to do with hospitality. Hospitality takes practice. We can practice giving hospitality and practice receiving it. We may never perfect it. It may never be easy. But we can practice it anyway, knowing that our Lord rejoices in our small beginnings.

THINKING IT THROUGH: What do you think would happen if you created a delicious, healthy meal for your guests instead of a pile of fat and calories? Do you think they would moan and complain that you don't love them anymore? Or would they still feel loved and nourished, especially if they knew you had created something healthy so you could have them in your life for longer?

PRAYER: Heavenly Father, thank you for Scripture which reminds us that a spirit of hospitality is something you desire for our hearts. Help me Holy Spirit to learn to show love to others and to receive love from others by what I say and do, in addition to what I eat. Thank you, Jesus for your example that truly showing love is by having a servant's heart. Help me develop a servant's heart today. Amen.

SMALL BEGINNINGS
Do you struggle with showing people love by feeding them? What little step can you do today to show love by feeding others healthier foods?

Chapter 8

Reasons We Overeat: The Bad

Do not let the devil get a foothold (Ephesians 4:7).

The context of Ephesians 4:7 is marriage. But let's face facts. We shouldn't let the devil get a foothold in any area of our lives. Bad eating for the bad reasons in this chapter has to do with eating for emotional reasons of procrastination and boredom and to change our physical or emotional state.

Procrastination

My son's favorite saying used to be "Getting started pays off in the long run but procrastination pays off now." Yes, it's funny, but not very helpful. Personally, I hate to put things off. It's as if that to-do list gets heavier as time passes. Plus, I *love* crossing off items on my to-do list.

I do however understand procrastination because there have been times where I have procrastinated out of fear. What if I don't do something right or well? The project is too big. I don't know where to start. My brain tells me why I can't do something when, if I didn't do all those brain exercises and just began, I'd be well into the project.

And that's the point. The solution to procrastination is to begin. Maybe you don't start at the best place. Maybe you don't know exactly what you're doing. But if you begin, then you soon understand where you need to go to find the best place to start. If you begin, you understand what you need to learn so that you know what you're doing.

Once you understand more about the scope of your project, you can break it down into manageable pieces and take them step by step, like a building project. Like rebuilding your temple.

The secret to not eating because of procrastination then is to just start doing what you're avoiding.

Eating from Boredom and Loneliness

Let's think about Ephesians again as it relates to boredom and loneliness. Are you ever bored? Do you just feel uninspired to do anything constructive? Do you watch too much TV or waste too much time on unproductive activities? Does boredom naturally lead you to want to do something with your hands—like shove food into your mouth?

Two areas of eating I fight are when watching TV and on long road trips. There's something about all that time I need to fill. It feels natural to fill it with food. Yeah, I know, there's nothing natural about it. So, what can I do?

For one thing, we finally made a house rule that there's no eating after 8:00 pm. Boy, that rule was tough in the beginning! We also try to turn off the TV in the evenings, play cards, sit outside and watch the stars or go for a walk around the block. But if we're watching TV, it's hard not to fall into mindless eating.

You know what I mean. You open a box of anything, intending to just have a small snack. Before you realize it, you're peering inside, wondering who ate the whole thing when you weren't looking.

Mindless eating can be a horrible thing. Not only from a health standpoint can it demolish your entire eating plan for the day, but it can set you back emotionally, discouraging you from even trying again.

Having a plan can help. Make a house rule about eating after a certain time. Then turn off the kitchen light. Or make a rule that there's no eating in front of the TV at all. Or make a rule that all eating must be done sitting at the kitchen table. Or at the very least, planning what you intend to eat can help. Then following through with that plan—measuring it out, putting the rest away, placing the allotted food onto a plate, sitting down, and fully focusing on enjoying it can help. In other words, making an intentional plan about eating is helpful.

Other people suggest working on something else. They suggest you keep your hands busy. If you're watching TV, knit or crochet. Or fiddle with a string of worry beads or rub a smooth rock. Or pet your dog. Or invite your cat onto your lap. Or brush your teeth so nothing will taste good anyway. But pay attention to what you're doing. Make what you do *intentional* is the suggestion.

Others advise that if you're lonely, get involved. Email a friend. Better yet, call her up and chat. Everyone busy? Get in your car and go to the mall or a church gathering or have a gathering of your own. Find people who are even more alone than you are. Being with them will take the focus off yourself and give you both something to be grateful for. God filled this world up with a whole bunch of people. "Find some" is the advice.

Reasons We Overeat: The Bad

Food Changes our Physical and Emotional States

All of us use food to change our physical state. If we are hungry, we eat, and the hunger goes away. If we eat for emotional reasons, we think food will ease our pain. We recognize that eating does in fact make us feel better, emotionally and physically. It does this emotionally by the pleasure we receive. It does this physically by altering the chemistry of our bodies.

Research tells us that carbohydrate-heavy comfort foods create serotonins—the neurotransmitter that contributes to a feeling of well-being. But while we may feel better in the immediate, short term, we know that eating less-than-nutritious comfort food is unhealthy. That understanding can give us a heavy sense of failure, which is often the opposite of a feeling of well-being.

Sometimes we eat because we are tired or are feeling physically drained. We may not be getting adequate sleep or are otherwise physically stressed. So, we fill up our energy tank with food. If we first grab simple sugars to get that quick spurt of energy, we may find that our energy level crashes an hour later.

For many people, that means it's time for another dose of simple sugars for more energy. Followed by another crash. And more simple sugars. For many people, the result is a cycle of craving and crashing.

Cravings and Addictive Eating

Some of us struggle with physical cravings for certain types of foods. And when we aren't eating them, we crave them, in greater and greater amounts. For me, the physical cravings are always simple carbohydrates. Such addictive foods often make us feel like we are constantly fighting temptation. Look at what Paul has to say about temptation:

> *No temptation has seized you except what is common to man. And God is faithful; he will not let you be tempted beyond what you can bear. But when you are tempted, he will also provide a way out so that you can stand up under it* (1 Corinthians 10:13).

God provides us with a way out of our temptations when it comes to eating, too. He provided us with prayer. He provided us with brains to figure out strategies to help us. He provided us with healthy foods as alternatives to unhealthy, addictive ones. He gave us friends and family who can encourage and support us. And He gave us the Holy Spirit to be our constant counselor, guide, and friend. In other words, He provided many ways for us to stand up under temptation.

Rather than a quick, but temporary energy fix from sugars, my doctors over the years have suggested that I feed my body protein and complex carbohydrates in the same meal. It takes longer for the energy fix to kick in, but the fix generally lasts longer, too, without a related craving and crash cycle.

On days when I am lacking energy, the most important and loving thing I can do for my health is to push the sugar and flour out of sight and grab hold of protein and complex carbohydrates.

Talk with your doctor or dietician and understand what might work best for you. Then figure out how you can lovingly provide the best fuel for your particular energy tank.

When Compulsive Eating and Addictive Eating Combine

Compulsive eating (just eating whatever; whenever for no particular reason) is different from addictive eating (physical craving for certain food groups). Addictive eating of junk food and compulsive, mindless eating, however, are often tied together. For example, most of the time, we don't find ourselves mindlessly eating Brussels sprouts or noshing on a head of cabbage. One thing we can do therefore is look at how the two types of eating often go together, by looking at **behavior, food choices, and portion control.**

For example, when my husband and I were settling on a rule about TV eating, we tried to determine if our TV eating was a *behavior* we wanted to change (mindless consumption of calories) or whether it had to do with *what we ate* while watching TV (addictive junk food).

In the end it didn't matter which reason it was. The fact was that eating while watching TV was the place it happened. By removing the opportunity to eat in that situation, we took away the opportunity for compulsive eating as well as eating addictive foods.

I'm pretty sure the Lord rejoiced at that small beginning.

THINKING IT THROUGH: List the people, places, and situations that trigger the types of emotional eating discussed in this chapter. Post your list somewhere you will see it. Focus on the fact that those triggers are less important than your health. Or that if you jeopardize your health by emotionally eating when triggered, you are jeopardizing your health, which itself adds more stress to your life.

PRAYER: Heavenly Father, thank you for giving me emotions. Help me focus on the good emotions like love, kindness, nobility, gentleness, and on what is true. Holy Spirit speak your truth loudly so your voice echoes inside my head. Amen.

SMALL BEGINNINGS
To what type of emotional eating could you apply Ephesians 4:7? What strategy might you use to stop your emotional eating?

Chapter 9

Reasons We Overeat: The Ugly

...seek first his kingdom and his righteousness, and all these things will be given to you as well. Therefore do not worry about tomorrow, for tomorrow will worry about itself. Each day has enough trouble of its own (Matthew 6:33-34).

It's hard to admit that we eat for emotional reasons. It's much easier to say we eat because of hunger. That's a physical issue of how our bodies deal with food. But an emotional issue is something I should have more control over. Me and the Holy Spirit. And I'm pretty sure the Holy Spirit isn't the one with the emotional food issues.

When I was writing these chapters, then, I had to face a major realization: I sometimes eat for emotional reasons that have nothing to do with fueling my body. The recognition of emotionally induced eating is a start. We looked briefly at eating out of procrastination, boredom, loneliness, cravings, and compulsion. But what should we do when we want to eat for the emotional reasons of worry and stress?

Let's settle first on some basic definitions. My definition is that worry is a chronic emotional state over something. For example, worry might center on the long-term health of a loved one or a divorce or financial crisis.

Stress, on the other hand could be defined as the feeling of "I need to," although stress may be related to a larger worry. For example, stress over getting a loved one to endless doctors' appointments could be related to a larger worry over that loved one's health. On the other hand, stress could simply be trying to fit life into 24 short hours in the day.

The bad news is that worry and stress often go together. That may mean two triggers for emotional eating. Let's address each one separately.

Worry Related Eating

The Bible is filled with Scripture telling us not to worry. Philippians 4:6-7 should be my life verse!

> *"Do not worry over anything but with prayer and petition, with thanksgiving present your requests to God. And the peace that transcends understanding will fill your heart and mind with Christ Jesus."*

I wish this verse was tattooed on my forehead—backwards—so every time I look in a mirror, I'd see it staring back at me. Instead I've memorized it. Whenever I'm tempted to eat out of worry, my goal is to stop everything and thank God that He is in control.

That can certainly help. Unfortunately, I have a mighty active imagination. That means I create *what-if* scenarios for things I imagine might or might not happen in the future. Once I create those scenarios, I start to worry over them in earnest. Instead of dealing with life as it is, I try to figure out any and every possible thing that could happen and the 53,271 things I should or should not do when they do.

Fortunately, the Apostle Paul had more to say in Philippians, just following the verse above. Read on to Paul's "whatever" verses:

> *Finally, brothers, whatever is true, whatever is noble, whatever is right, whatever is pure, whatever is lovely, whatever is admirable—if anything is excellent or praiseworthy—think about such things* (Philippians 4:8).

Did you notice that very first *whatever* we are told to think about? We're told to think about whatever is true. Hang on a minute! I'm much more skilled at thinking up *what if's*! But those *what ifs* have not actually happened. They only exist in my imagination. In other words, those *what if's* are *not true.*

I didn't need to read any further in Philippians to understand this revelation. For years I had focused on endless made-up lists of *what if's,* having failed to memorize Paul's *whatevers.* All I need to remember is Paul's very first *whatever.* In other words, I just needed not to think about what was not true.

I could then focus on what *is true*—the good things I had going for me. Those are the noble, right, pure, lovely, admirable, excellent, and praiseworthy things. Once we stop conjuring up imaginary *what ifs*, we can start counting blessings.

Scripture—as always—provides the perfect advice for whatever we are going through; whatever we are worrying about. Whatever.

Stress Related Eating

Stress can also be a trigger that causes us to overeat or eat badly. Scripture also recognizes our tendency to feel stress in our lives; often because we feel rushed or pressured or incapable of getting everything done—on time or well.

> *Who of you by worrying can add a single hour to his life?* (Matthew 6:27).

Yes, that Scripture uses the word "worry" rather than "stress." But it might be that your worry is actually stress from simply having too few hours in the day. So, let's apply Matthew 6:27 to stress. It then reads, "Who of you by stressing about not having enough time in the day, can add a single hour to it?"

Oh, the truth of it. Do what you can, when you can do it, and do it the best way you can. Leave the rest to God, knowing you have been a faithful steward of the time He has given you.

What can you do for short term stress? Is your stress a "today-only" kind of stress? If so, it will pass. We can thank God that tomorrow might be brighter. We can ask the Holy Spirit to handle the stress for us and remember also that in terms of stress-induced eating, if we eat too much food or the wrong kinds of food now out of stress, we will only feel *more* stressed by our failure to manage it.

We can remember also that exercise releases stress. Are you able to get up right now and go for a walk? Can you stand up, twist a few times at the waist, stretch your arms and breathe deeply? Where do you carry your stress? In your stomach? Your neck and head? Your shoulders? Listen to your body and focus on where you are feeling stress right now.

A great exercise given me by a physician when stress is in your stomach starts with closing your eyes. Push your stomach muscles out as far as they will go. Breathe slowly and deeply several times. Chances are those stomach muscles are clenched tight. By pushing our stomachs out, we're forcing them to unclench. By breathing deeply, we're counteracting the shallow breathing we typically fall into when stressed.

Are you carrying stress in your neck and head? A chiropractor told me that we often tense our neck muscles when we're stressed. When those neck muscles tighten, they constrict the blood vessels that take blood to our brains. The result may be a headache. Relaxing those neck muscles and breathing deeply might help. His suggestion is to roll your head in circles a few times. Take several deep breaths. Massage your neck.

Similarly, if you are carrying stress in your shoulders, close your eyes and breathe deeply. Shrug your shoulders up and down. Roll them in circles. Lift your arms and swing them around. Release the tension in those shoulder muscles. Feel better?

Don't quite know where you are carrying the stress? A masseuse says to slip off your shoes and massage your feet. Close your eyes and feel the relaxation pour into you. If you imagine the nerves that run throughout your body, your feet are the end. And since the nerves then head back up from your feet, they are also the beginning of your nerves—heading to all parts of your body again.

What can you do for long-term stress and worry? If your stress or worry is something you live with every day of your life, then you need to ask yourself what you can do to change your circumstances. Or who you can ask for help. Or share it with a friend. Or seek counseling or meditation. Or medication. If your physical health is suffering from long-term stress, eating because of that stress will not solve anything. It will only give you another area of your health you will need to address (and stress over) later.

My friend Bonnie is rebuilding her temple after a heart attack. She shared these steps from her stress management class.

1. Choose one realistic outcome you would like to achieve

2. Assess your level of motivation from one to ten

3. What specific steps are needed to achieve this goal: what, when, where, how much, how often?

4. What may be a barrier to achieving that goal?

5. How will I address and overcome this barrier?

6. What/who are my resources or supports?

My wise friend, Bonnie added another step based on Romans 8:1.

> There is now therefore no condemnation for those who love Christ Jesus.

In other words, Bonnie's advice is to not condemn yourself. If you hit a bump in the road, get back on the bike and keep peddling one crank of the wheel at a time. Remember that the Lord rejoices in small beginnings—even if we have to begin those beginnings again and again.

If you can't do anything else, take your long-term stress or worry one day at a time. Turn it into short-term stress. Then take life one day at a time; one moment at a time. Focus on doing what you can do when you can do it.

Now what?

Once we recognize we may be eating for emotional reasons, what can we do about it? Boredom we can do something about by doing something. That goes for procrastination, too. As well as loneliness.

Cravings and addictive eating we can manage by not beginning the cycle; by carefully selecting the first foods we eat each morning and throughout the day.

We can manage energy levels by similarly selecting foods that provide us long-term energy and stamina and striving to get adequate sleep.

We can avoid compulsive eating by becoming aware of when and where we are most likely to eat mindlessly.

With all forms of emotional eating, one thing we can do is interrupt the emotion/food connection. Perhaps making a list of things that might help you interrupt the pattern when you are tempted to eat when not hungry will help you. Here's my list. What can *you* do?

- Brush my teeth
- Chew gum
- Take a shower or soak in the tub
- Lie down for a rest
- Read a book (the Bible is a good one!)
- Call a friend
- Write in a journal
- Take a walk
- Play with the dog
- Do laundry

Best of all, the Holy Spirit is there with you; in you, ready to be your counselor and comforter. God will provide a way out of your temptation so you can stand up under it. Give it to God and watch what He does with it.

I have not addressed emotional eating issues of binging, anorexia, bulimia or eating due to depression. These eating disorders may be the result of true physiological problems with your body's chemistry or deeper psychological issues that require counseling or medication. Professional help may be the foundational building block you need to begin or complete your rebuilding process. Please obtain it.

THINKING IT THROUGH: List the types of worry or stress you go through on a regular basis. Are there specific worries or stresses or do you simply feel a general sense of overall anxiety?

What can you do to lessen your worry or stress? Can you try the simple techniques in this chapter? If so, how did they help? If they didn't, what might you try or who might be able to help you?

Have you fully released your burdens to your Heavenly Father in prayer? Do you need to continually release them daily? Do not give up on your Heavenly Father. He will not give up on you.

PRAYER: Heavenly Father, help me focus only on what is true. Jesus, thank you for being the voice of truth. Speak your truth loudly, Holy Spirit, so your voice echoes inside my head over the *whatifs* I am inventing. Amen.

SMALL BEGINNINGS
What things do you regularly worry about or stress over? Which of the Apostle Paul's *whatevers* might you be able to apply to those issues?

Chapter 10

Eat with a Grateful Heart

Be joyful always; pray continually; give thanks in all circumstances, for this is God's will for you in Christ Jesus (1 Thessalonians 5:16-18).

When I first began the idea of writing *Rebuild Your Tattered Temple* it was little more than a journal. How have I done rebuilding since I began that journal? I started to write, "horribly!" But that is a negative comment and this chapter is about living with a grateful heart. If you have a grateful heart, a natural result should be a positive attitude.

One thing I have learned over the years is that I am not as naturally positive as I thought. Yes, I always have a song going through my head and those songs keep me cheerful inside. But on the *outside*, I moan and groan. A lot.

Recently someone I thought of as enormously negative made the comment that he was "a positive person." It was such an outrageous comment for him to make. But then it hit me.

Maybe all of us believe we are positive. Outwardly, however, we often display negativity through our actions or comments or our reactions to life. No matter how positive we think we are, those outward things we say and do affect our internal perceptions as well.

There is a familiar saying that if you say something long enough and loud enough, people will believe it. Well, could it be that if you say and do enough negative things often enough, *you* will become negative, too, no matter what happy little ditty is playing inside your head? Since what we think and do affects our future success, we should do and say, as well as think—positively.

Once I began to monitor myself more closely, I discovered—drat! I *do* sound more negative than I feel. Even when I'm joking, if there's a negative component to my comment, it can have negative results internally. Think of all the times we say, "I can't, "I don't want to," "I have to."

In short, I need to—oops—I *want* to focus on restating these comments with "I get to," I choose to," and "I want to."

It's a daily struggle to focus on the positive. The first step is realization of what you're doing and saying. So, are you saying things that come out more negative than you feel? Is it helping you defeat your efforts to rebuild your temple?

One thing my mom taught me was to say thank you. When someone gives me a gift, a thank you card gets sent. When a door is opened for me, a thank you is said. And when we sit down to eat the gift of God's bountiful food, He deserves a thank you.

It's called grace, because it's what *we get*. We're not giving God grace. God *is* grace! He gives grace to us—something we receive that we don't deserve.

When we say grace, then, we're acknowledging the gift from God that we don't deserve; thanking Him for the gift of food that we need in order to be able to accept His grace in all areas of our lives.

The number one definition of grace listed in Webster's is "unmerited divine assistance given humans for their regeneration or sanctification." Did you notice the words "unmerited," "divine" and "regeneration"? When applied to salvation, we understand that we certainly don't deserve it, it's a gift from God, and because of salvation we will spend eternity divinely regenerated in heaven.

When applied to food, grace reminds us that

- We don't deserve it just because we exist

- It's from God, and

- We need it for our physical regeneration. To rebuild these temples.

Did you grow up saying grace before meals? I did. Except that somehow over the years, grace became what we did in a group over our evening meal. Somehow breakfast eaten at the counter or munching on a protein bar on the way to work didn't count as an official meal and therefore didn't require an official thank you.

How's that for logic?

And somehow if we're eating lunch in a restaurant surrounded by unbelievers, surely God doesn't expect us to bow our heads and give thanks.

Of course, He does.

I confess I sometimes forget to say grace, especially when I'm eating alone. The truth is that I forget I'm not really alone. God is right there with me, blessing the food He created and waiting for a simple, heartfelt thank you. From our point of view, saying grace is a reminder to live and eat with a grateful heart.

How does saying grace and living in gratitude affect our rebuilding efforts? For one thing, it reminds us to stop and enjoy the food we are eating; to pay attention to it and in doing so to stop ourselves from mindless, unhealthy eating or simple overeating.

For another thing, saying grace reinforces a positive attitude in all areas of life. The more positive we are the more likely we are to feel that we *can* accomplish our goals and do so with a song in our heart and a smile on our face.

More importantly, saying grace keeps our hearts attuned to God. The more attuned we are, the more the Holy Spirit is empowered to do those things that are His job to do: guide, encourage, counsel, lead.

Mom nagged me to always say thank you and Dad nagged me to not talk with my mouth full. Taken together, my parents taught me to do what pleases our Heavenly Father: to say grace *before* I take that first bite; to live in gratitude for the bounty God has given.

THINKING IT THROUGH: Do you think you are a positive person? What things run through your head during the day? Are you singing songs or are you rehearsing arguments you plan to have? Do you have an "I need to" or an "I want to" speech pattern? Monitor your thoughts and speech for a day. If you need to change, how can you do it? Take every thought and word "captive" (2 Corinthians 10:5).

PRAYER: Heavenly Father, thank you for being my great provider. Thank you for your food, the nutrition it provides, and the pleasure it brings. Help me eat with praise on my lips so there is less time to shove in food I don't need and less room to say words that do not encourage others and myself.

Please use this fuel, Holy Spirit, to rebuild your temple. Help me work with you to grow this body into the best, healthiest, most energetic, and most beautiful body I can so that I can better do your work, Jesus, in this world. Amen.

SMALL BEGINNINGS
Start a gratitude journal. How might 1 Thessalonians 5:16-18 and Philippians 4:6-7 help you focus on gratitude rather than bad reasons for overeating?

Chapter 11

Savoring Food

Why spend money on what is not bread, and your labor on what does not satisfy? Listen, listen to me, and eat what is good, and your soul will delight in the richest of fare" (Isaiah 55:2).

God made us to enjoy eating. If that were not so, He could have simply created beige wafers for us to eat. Think of the poor baleen whales, which have no teeth. All they get to eat forever are gigantic, gorging gulps of microscopic plankton. Well, plankton and an occasional disobedient minister sent by God to preach to Nineveh.

Food is basically fuel so our bodies can function. But praise God! He made our food taste good, too. Food tasting good is part of that abundant living Jesus spoke about. It's also about our God who richly provides us with everything for our enjoyment (1 Timothy 6:17).

We enjoy food. Some of us have enjoyed it so much that our temples are now bulging. But here is something to think about. Is the enjoyment of food really the cause of our problem? Or do we eat too much and too much of the wrong things because we *fail* to fully enjoy the food we eat?

What?

We've talked about choices of food—eating the perfect food God created for us and the bounty He created to choose from. We've also talked about eating enough but not too much. So, what do I mean when I ask if we eat too much because we fail to fully enjoy what we eat?

I mean, that even if we're eating God's food, we may not be getting the sensual pleasure from it that God intended us to have. If part of the reason we eat is to fully enjoy our food, eating without paying attention, may mean it takes us longer to get to that point of satisfaction. Maybe we can reach the point of satisfaction and consume less food if we truly enjoy it as it's going down the little red lane.

Let's look at the way God created us to taste. Not only does food taste either good or bad. It also tastes sweet and sour and salty and bitter and bland and spicy.

If we held a small lemon and a large lime in our hands while we were blindfolded, we might not be able to tell the difference between them through touch. But, still blindfolded, we can instantly taste the difference between a lemon and a lime even though the texture of the fruit on the tongue is similar, they're both slightly sweet, slightly tart, and slightly acidic.

Even when a food dish is made with a combination of ingredients, we can pick out the separate flavors. Think sweet and sour chicken over rice. We can taste the sweet sugar. We can taste the sour vinegar. We can taste the salty soy sauce. We can taste the specific flavor of meat. We can taste the nutty brown rice and tell that it's not the white, sticky kind. We can taste the spicy green peppers, the hot onions, and the individual flavors of the water chestnuts, carrots, and celery.

God created thousands of tiny patches on our tongues so we could differentiate each and every one of those flavors. It would have been simpler for God to just stick a floppy pink tongue in our mouths to help us get the food down our throats.

But our God took the time and care to create thousands of taste buds that give us the ability to appreciate the variety of tastes He created. Our sense of taste is part of our enjoyment of food.

But taste is only one of the senses God created to let us enjoy food. Another part of tasting is smell. Have you ever lost your sense of smell, maybe when you were ill, and your nose was so stopped up you couldn't breathe out of it? When that happens, the food just doesn't taste as good.

We might have said we lost our appetite. But often part of losing our appetite is because we've lost our sense of smell. Think about the times when you walked into a room and smelled fresh bread cooling on a rack. Part of the delight you had in taking that first bite was the aroma. Our sense of smell is part of our enjoyment of food.

God also gave us the sense of sight. Have you ever sat down to a dinner and noticed your mouth watering just looking at the food? A watering mouth is God's way of getting your mouth prepared for the eating process. And how much more enjoyment do we ladies have sitting down to a beautifully set table with placemats that match the napkins, flowers in the center, elegant china and crystal goblets gleaming in the candlelight? For many women, the more beautiful the food *looks*, the better it tastes. The sense of sight prepares us for the taste. It's part of the enjoyment of food.

Savoring Food

God also gave us the sense of touch. God created broccoli to be velvety when cooked but bristly when raw. He created nuts to be dry and oranges juicy. He created carrots to crunch and milk to be creamy. Some foods are hard; some soft; some chewy; some mushy. Some foods are eaten hot; some are cold; some in between. Temperature, too, is part of our sense of touch. Imagine if God had intended us to get all of our nutrition from room temperature liquid. We might be desperate for something to really sink our teeth into and crunch, crunch, crunch. The sense of touch is also part of the enjoyment of food.

Speaking of crunching, God also gave us a sense of hearing. There's a satisfying sound we hear when we crunch and chew and lick and slurp our food. Think kids eating spaghetti. Picture the look of disappointment on their faces when you tell them to stop slurping. Listen to the smacking sound when you chew with your mouth open. It may not be pleasurable to your dining companion, but admit it gals, you sometimes do it when you're alone, right? That smacking sound is pure enjoyment.

And even if you're politely chewing with your mouth closed, isn't it awesome that God placed our ears right there above our jaws? We get to listen to ourselves chewing even if nobody else can hear. What if God had placed our ears down on our feet? We wouldn't have that great satisfaction of listening to the sound of food being crunched and smooshed. The sense of hearing is also part of the enjoyment of food.

When was the last time you really, fully enjoyed God's food, using all your senses? Is it more likely that you shovel food into your mouth without taking the time to appreciate it fully? One benefit of savoring is that your body will have time for your stomach to tell your brain it's full. As a result, nutrition experts tell us you may eat less food. Equally important though, by more fully appreciating your food, you may also feel *satisfied* with less because you have received more pleasure from it.

God made our temple capable of enjoying pleasure. It's part of God's plan to enjoy food. Tasty food is His gift and He created us to enjoy it fully. So, go ahead and enjoy your food to the fullest; abundantly—not in volume but in degree. Praise God that He richly provides everything for our enjoyment.

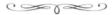

THINKING IT THROUGH: Do you take time to savor your food? What could you do to increase the sensual experience of eating? Could you arrange it nicely on a table setting? Could you make sure to include several colors of food on your plate? Could you combine contrasting flavors and textures? Do you need to turn off a TV or stop doing another activity so you can focus on your food?

After you say grace and before you take your first bite, try this: really look at your food. What interesting things do you see that you never noticed before? See how that kernel of brown rice has split open? Imagine it has burst because it is filled with too many nutrients and too much flavor to be contained.

Pick up a forkful of food. Close your eyes and smell the aroma. Still with your eyes closed, put the food into your mouth. Let your tongue roll it around in your mouth before you begin to chew. Notice the texture and the temperature. Can you separate the various tastes? Is it salty, sweet, bitter, acidic? A combination?

Now chew your food and notice how the texture and flavor changes. After you swallow, take a sip of water and try a forkful of another food on your plate. Spend the time to enjoy the sensual pleasures of food that God created.

PRAYER: Father God, thank you for the bounty of food and drink you have given us—both for the nutrition and the sensual experience of it. Thank you for the taste, smell, color, texture, and sound of your foods. Help me experience and appreciate that not only have you given me food for sustenance, but for my pleasure as well. Amen.

SMALL BEGINNINGS
What one thing can you do today to savor your food and experience more satisfaction from it?

Chapter 12

Reworking Recipes

Therefore, salt is good; but if even salt has become tasteless, with what will it be seasoned? (Luke 14:34).

Jesus is the spice of our life. We may be the salt of the earth, but Jesus is sweet cinnamon; tingling pepper, sizzling curry, and smooth basil. If we lose our saltiness and become tasteless in living our faith, what we need is Jesus to spice it up again.

When I was thinking about the topic of reworking recipes, this Scripture about salt immediately came to mind. Taken literally, we know that too much salt can harm our health. We of course need some salt in our diets.

Without getting too science-y, salt helps us absorb other nutrients. It helps regulate water balance. It helps our nerves work properly. It preserves the acid-base balance in our body, helps digestive stomach acid, works with potassium absorption, and helps our blood carry carbon dioxide to the lungs. We lose salt when we sweat. Then we need to replenish that salt.

Reworking Recipes

Animals will travel miles to locate a naturally occurring deposit of minerals to lick the salt from it. People also will set out a chunk of salt for cattle and to attract wild deer. We know that salt is essential for life.

But not too much salt.

If our doctor has told us to lower the salt in our diet, one of the ways we can do so is to rework our recipes by replacing salt with something else that tastes even better. Just like God created a variety of food, He also created a variety of spices. Next time you're at the grocery store check out the spice aisle. Notice the store often alphabetizes the spices so you can find one amid the dozens on multiple shelves. And those ones are just a few of the spices available. Ever go to an Indian spice shop or an Asian grocery? God sure has an imagination!

Keeping spices in mind, we can look at our recipes as chemical formulas and create new food experiments.

For example, if you typically include salt in a recipe, you might try using oregano, basil, turmeric or coriander instead. Or use half the salt and fill in the other half with spices.

If you're super eager to experiment, when making your recipe, you can divide it into several parts and try one or two new spices in each portion, replacing some or all of the salt. Then present the dishes to your family and have them vote on which result they prefer. Make it fun.

In fact, get out all of your spices and set them on the counter. It's just a little clutter. Leave them out where you can see them and *use* them! Try them. One at a time. Combine two or three. Try a different one next time with the same recipe or a different one.

Reworking Recipes

Sugar and white flour are my problem. Moving from simple to complex carbohydrates is therefore very important for me. One thing we can do is to simply reduce the amount of white sugar in a recipe and switch from processed white flour to a whole grain flour or almond flour.

Thinking about making grandma's famous war cake with buttermilk frosting out of wheat flour may just sound like we're desecrating her name! Would she roll over in her grave? Or would she watch you turn her prize-winning bucket of sweet love into something healthy and then run around bragging to the angels what her smart granddaughter just came up with?

Can you substitute some of the sugar with raisins or applesauce or smashed bananas or add a hefty amount of cinnamon to tantalize the taste buds?

Fat is another problem for many people. We now have many trans-fat free fats we can use in cooking. But although one fat may not equal another fat in health consequences, too much fat in general can still be a health issue for some people. If it is for you, how can you reduce the amount of bad fat in your diet by substituting good fat? And how can you lower your overall fat in your diet?

You may need to determine if you need to focus on a specific fat. Do you consume too much high-cholesterol fat in the form perhaps of whole butter, high-fat dairy products or higher fat animal products? Can you substitute one of the new trans-fat-free; hydrogenated fat-free margarines for butter?

Or can you start by whipping the margarine and butter together to lower the bad fat?

Can you switch from whole milk to 2% milk and then to 1% milk and then to skim? Or mix half skim and half 1%?

Reworking Recipes

Can you switch from regular ice cream to low fat ice cream or low-fat yogurt and make it low in sugar, too?

What can you do?

Can you switch from sautéing your veggies in butter, to sautéing them in olive oil? Or even better, can you switch to a non-stick pan and add herbs and spices to substitute for the butter flavor?

If you need to work on lowering the amount of higher fatty animal products, what can you do?

Can you use low fat ground turkey or chicken instead of hamburger or sausage?

Can you select the leanest beef available? If cost is prohibitive, can you buy it anyway but split one serving between two people and then focus on really enjoying it?

Can you use meat as an additive to food instead of making it the main focus of the meal, for example, by dicing the meat and adding it to a brown rice and veggie dish rather than serving it as a slab that takes up three-quarters of the plate?

Can you plan your meals in advance to allow yourself one special meal each week of very lean beef or lean pork tenderloin and surround that meal with alternating days of chicken, fish, seafood, and turkey?

Can you include in your weekly meal plan one meatless day getting protein from beans, tofu, egg whites or low-fat cheese? In fact, can you regularly use egg whites in all your recipes instead of whole eggs?

What about other ingredients you use in cooking?

Can you over time reduce the amount of white pasta and white rice you use and increase the amount of whole grains and brown rice? Or cauliflower instead of rice or mashed potatoes? Or spiralized zucchini instead of spaghetti noodles?

Can you add snippets of shredded veggies at first until over time your recipes are more veggies than grains or meats?

What can you do to reinvent your family's favorite recipes and turn them into temple-building blocks?

Portion control is another problem for many people. How can you adjust your recipes to address that issue? Make smaller amounts? Make the same amount but divide it into two and freeze one part for another day?

If making cookies, can you use a melon baller to make small cookies instead of rolling them into hefty ones? Can you freeze most of your cookies in smaller packages and stuff them at the back of your freezer where you'll have to work to get at them?

What is your problem? One of these? All of them? Something entirely different? Be honest with yourself. Think about what you need to do and then think about what you *can* do. Then…

…do it.

THINKING IT THROUGH: What is your biggest problem in cooking healthier recipes? Think of your very favorite foods— either ones you buy premade or ones you make yourself. What can you do to re-create that recipe and turn it into something healthy? When you sit down with your family to taste your new creation, do so with joy. Don't think *this will be a poor substitution for what I really want.* Instead think, *if I make it right and eat it in the proper amounts, I can truly have my cake and eat it, too!* Praise God for that.

PRAYER: Heavenly Father, thank you for creating so much variety in our lives. As I contemplate how I can do something today to improve my eating habits, please release imagination into my life. Open up my cupboards and show me how to use the abundance of flavor you have provided to rebuild my temple by what I eat. Give me a commitment and resolve to do my part today. Amen.

SMALL BEGINNINGS
What favorite family recipe calls to you to be reworked? How might you make a healthier version of it?

Part IV

Body Mechanics

Chapter 13

Letting Your Body Work as it Should

But in fact God has placed the parts in the body, every one of them, just as he wanted them to be. If they were all one part, where would the body be? As it is, there are many parts, but one body (1 Corinthians 12:18-20).

"Stand up straight!"

It's time to concede the truth my mother tried to impart all those years: posture is important. Not only have all those "perfect posture" muscles atrophied over the years, but a saggy posture just makes me *feel* saggy.

One of our focuses for this chapter then is to sit, stand, and walk tall and proud for Jesus. And while we're doing so, here's a variation on Scripture for us girls.

*Therefore, **my dear sisters**, stand firm. Let nothing move you **(except exercise)**. Always give yourselves fully to the work of the Lord **(in rebuilding your temple)**, because you know that your labor in the*

Letting Your Body Work as it Should

Lord is not in vain (1 Corinthians 15:58; emphasis and explanation mine).

We are called to stand firm for Christ. And from a physical point of view, we are to stand tall and straight to allow the organs and muscles in our bodies work as God intended them to work.

Body mechanics though is more than just standing correctly. A few years ago, I developed horrible pain in my lower back. Somewhere along the years, as I fell asleep, I swung my top leg out in front of me, with the inner knee resting on the mattress. Then I tucked my toes around and under my other knee. I know. You can't even imagine what this would look like.

The top half of my body was lying sideways but my bottom half was stomach sleeping. The place where my body went from side to front is where the pain centered. I had to re-train myself to sleep in a better position.

Are you doing something similar? Do you wake with backaches? Think through your sleeping position. Do you need to change it? If you wake with pain in the hips, do you need to place a pillow between your knees to better align your hips? If you wake with numbness in your arms or hands, are you restricting blood flow by how you position your arms during sleep? If you have pain on waking, you may need to pay attention to the body mechanics at work while you sleep. Sleeping is supposed to be a time when your body rests and restores itself, not a time to make your body feel worse.

Another area of concern for women approaching or exceeding the half century mark, is our knees. Those babies help us walk, sit, and dance. And they should be used extensively for prayer. They're dog-gone important joints. But they're also one of the first joints to decay. The most important thing we can do to relieve stress on our knees is to lose a few pounds. What else can we do to help our knees work better for longer?

Think about the type of exercise you do. Some forms of exercise are extra strenuous on the knees and can make existing conditions worse. For example, if the cartilage in your knees rubs against each other, talk to your doctor and discuss the best choice of exercise for you.

Do you need to work on strengthening the muscles that support your knees? Then find exercises that help and start doing them slowly, so the muscles are built up rather than the knees broken down.

How do you rise out of a chair? Do you need to push off the seat with your arms or push on your knees with your hands as you rise to help take some of the stress off your knees? Then do it.

If you sit at a computer all day, chances are you have developed other aches and pains. Perhaps your fingers, hands, wrists and lower arms have developed pains or numbness. Can you adjust your chair or your positioning to improve your body mechanics? Do you have neck or upper back pain? Then take a look at how you are sitting, the height of your chair in relation to the computer and monitor and your head placement. Can you focus on repositioning yourself to improve your body mechanics?

When we were children, we could twist and turn and spin and whirl, do cartwheels and splits. It was just a few of those things kids did. Now some days we're just happy to be able to get up without collapsing into a heap on the floor.

But we can think about the way we carry ourselves throughout the day. How can we carry ourselves in the way God created our bodies to move? If we're generally moving well, then how can we do what we do with more gusto? How can we move our muscles and limbs in the same way we have been but move them better or with more energy?

One thing we can do is to be conscious of how we are moving our bodies and how they are supposed to move. We can recognize that God created our bodies to be well-oiled machines. It's our job to keep them moving in the way they were created.

Spiritually, we were made to worship God. And, yes, He gave us awesome knees so we could bow down in praise while pouring our hearts out to Him in prayer. God wants us to move spiritually as well as physically in the way He intended.

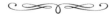

THINKING IT THROUGH: Have you ever thought about what your organs must feel like when you slouch? Your heart is saying, "squish, squash, squorsh" instead of its lively thump-ity-thump-thump."

Your lungs gasp, "Huuuuh! Huuuuh!" with every breath instead of the air flowing freely and easily inside like the flitting of butterfly wings.

We humans generally try to find the very easiest way to do everything. But we force our internal organs and muscles to work harder simply because we're not carrying ourselves properly. Let's embrace our laziness and stand up straight today!

PRAYER: Heavenly Father, thank you for designing this body to move. Forgive me when I don't move my body in the way you intended. Holy Spirit remind me to stand, sit, and move with energy and grace today and to use this body to do the will of the Father. Jesus thank you for your example of faithfulness. Amen.

SMALL BEGINNINGS
What aspect of how you stand, sit, walk or sleep do you do improperly? How might you focus on correcting that part of your body mechanics, so you feel and move better?

Chapter 14

God Breathes: Cardiovascular Exercise

Don't you realize that in a race everyone runs, but only one person gets the prize? So run to win! All athletes are disciplined in their training. They do it to win a prize that will fade away, but we do it for an eternal prize (1 Corinthians 9:24-25).

I was one of those crazy people who used to run before it was called "jogging." I'd slide into my white tennis shoes; tug on a pair of grey sweatpants, and off I'd go. No $200 running shoes. No fashionable jogging togs. Not even a sports bra, since there was no such thing back then. I had no particular style in my running. Certainly, I had no training and had no ambition to run a marathon or beat a record. I just knew that running made me feel good. It made me breathe. It made me strong.

Paul's running metaphor in 1 Corinthians may not speak to you. And some of us may no longer be in any condition to run. But all of us generally need regular aerobic (cardiovascular) exercise.

A dictionary definition of aerobics is that it is a system of physical conditioning designed to enhance circulatory and respiratory efficiency. It involves vigorous sustained exercise, such as jogging, swimming, or cycling. And doctors remind us that this form of aerobic exercise should be ongoing.

What happens when a body builder stops lifting weights? Those bulging muscles no longer bulge. They droop and sag.

Your heart is a muscle, too. Just like biceps, your heart needs to be worked so it can be strong and pump oxygen-rich blood from your lungs throughout your body. Doctors tell us that by aerobically conditioning our bodies, we increase our heart and lung capacity. We can get oxygen and nutrient-carrying blood to every part of our body more efficiently so that the rebuilding of our temple can take place better and faster.

None of us need a medical degree to recognize the benefits of cardiovascular exercise. But here are some we don't always think about.

1. Aerobic exercise makes us sweat. Sweat is one of the ways God created our bodies to rid ourselves of toxins. Sweating helps cleanse our skin. It also gives us a healthy glow. Glowing is good.

2. Aerobic exercise gives us energy. Hey, wait. If I go running, I'll be exhausted. Sure, you'd be tired if the first day you started you ran a marathon. But if you start walking for 5 minutes the first day and increasing weekly until you're walking a mile and finally running several miles over a period of weeks or months—you are building your strength and your stamina. More stamina means you have more energy for less strenuous activities in your life, like basic living.

3. The other reason why you have more energy is that you are getting more oxygen. Remember that thing about

increasing our heart and lung capacity? Think about what you do when you're tired. You yawn. The yawn may be triggered by something else, but the result is that yawning forces you to take in more oxygen.

4. Oxygen makes us feel more alert. One of the places our blood takes oxygen to is our brain. Our fuzzy head feels less fuzzy when we have enough oxygen feeding it. Think of it as God giving us artificial respiration.

5. Aerobic exercise also relieves stress. We've all heard that, and if you haven't experienced it personally, it's way past time you did. God created our bodies to need exercise for a whole bunch of reasons. And one reason evidently is to relieve stress. Stress can be a huge destroyer of our health. If we can't remove the *causes* or *sources* of the stress, we can do things to relieve the *effect* of stress, so it doesn't overwhelm us.

6. That leads to another benefit. Aerobic exercise encourages rest and relaxation. Not only can we fall asleep quicker if we don't have stress, but we can sleep better having worked our muscles during the day. The way we build muscles is by first tearing the muscles down. Then God does His miracle thing and repairs those tiny rips and tears during deep sleep at night, making the repairs even stronger than the muscles were before. In other words, the way we grow stronger is by first being torn down.

Hey, there's an opportunity for a spiritual discussion if I ever heard one! Go ahead, girls. Talk about that one for a while. I'll wait...

7. Another benefit of aerobic exercise is beauty. A healthy, fit body is a more beautiful body. It's lean and graceful. It's not a body that's hunched over, tired, and out of breath.

Come on, ladies! God intended us to be beautiful. One way to be as beautiful as you can be is to be as healthy as you can be.

Convinced? Let's think together about aerobic exercise, then and how to create a plan to do it.

Before you have a plan though you may need permission from your doctor. If your temple is really in bad shape, find out how much exercise your doctor thinks is a good beginning. You may just be starting out wagging your finger to the beat of music. But it'll be a start. Locate a reasonable place to begin and work up from there.

When creating your plan, remember to focus on getting your heart pumping and taking in oxygen. Oxygen is important. It cleanses our bodies and feeds our cells. Christ came to give us life so that we might live it abundantly, so breathe oxygen and *breathe* it in abundance.

Here are some different types of aerobic exercise:

- Dancing
- Jumping rope
- Jogging
- Walking
- Swimming
- Bicycling
- Tennis
- Rowing
- Ice skating
- Roller blading
- Martial arts

As for dancing, there's ballet, modern, cha-cha, salsa, ballroom, belly, flamingo, hula, and a couple thousand forms of cardio dancing on DVDs, available to slide right into your personal DVD player at home.

There are also dozens of exercise machines to encourage aerobic exercise, such as the elliptical trainer, treadmill, step climber, rowing machine, health rider, stationary bicycle. New machines are being invented daily. Pick something and get started.

But start by listening to your body and to your doctor. That means don't overdo it first thing. You don't want to have to take a break to recover. That would be backward motion. Keep moving forward while you're building up.

You might aim for an ultimate goal of a nice sweaty workout. I have a feeling that a sweaty body working for God's glory is a mighty pleasing aroma to God.

THINKING IT THROUGH: What type of aerobic exercise do you enjoy most? Is it something you can physically do even if you can't do it *well* right now? Do you need special equipment? If so, do you have it or have access to it? Or money to purchase it? Can you do this activity inside or outside or either one?

What things might prevent you from making this a year-round exercise option? If you can only do it part of the year, what alternative form of aerobic exercise can you do the rest of the year? Do you do better when exercising with other people? If so, who could you ask to join you? Focus on how you can make it happen.

PRAYER: Heavenly Father, thank you for breathing into me the breath of life. Help me, Holy Spirit to use this body in ways that build it up from the inside out. Jesus, give me strength to run the race—both physically and spiritually—for you. Amen.

SMALL BEGINNINGS
The Books of Genesis and John speak of God literally breathing life and spirit into humans.
How might this inspire you in terms of your health?

Chapter 15

Christ Strengthens Me: Strength Exercise

Therefore, strengthen your feeble arms and weak knees. "Make level paths for your feet," so that the lame may not be disabled, but rather healed (Hebrews 12:12).

When I was 20, I started lifting weights. I had all the equipment—weight bench, bar bells, free weights (back when they were called "dumbbells"). I didn't lift weights to develop muscles or be manly. It was just part of my overall exercise routine. I seemed to have been much smarter in my youth.

Now I praise God when my son comes home so he can open my pickle jar!

My point is that I'm not strong anymore. You know those flappy things you get about age 45 that hang down from just below your armpits? Got 'em. You know those perky little things that used to stand up firmly on your chest? Droopy.

Maybe your big goal isn't to be tight all over. Maybe your initial focus is weight loss. Well, if that's your goal, baby, I got news for you! Exercise experts tell us that muscles burn more calories than flab. In other words, to burn more calories we have to build up our muscles. That's strength training, girlfriend. Lifting weights.

"I barely have time for the aerobics program I started in the last chapter!" you say. Well, girlfriend, are you walking? Then grab some hand weights and swing them around while you walk. Lift them high. Across your body. Behind your back. Figure out how you can make this work for *you*.

Believe me when I tell you that after I decided to include strength training in my present exercise program, I was a weak Nelly. Hot-flash induced hand waving was the only exercise I got. So, did I start out pumping 30-pound weights? Puh-lease.

I began with 3-pound weights which look more like thick pencils than any sort of exercise equipment. I explained to the clerk at the sporting goods store that they were for an elderly woman. Okay, so I meant *this* elderly woman, but I had to get out of there with some semblance of self-respect, right?

I settled on six basic exercises. I made sure I knew how to do them properly. Then I set up my program. Wanna see it?

Week 1: 3-pound weights. Two sets of six repetitions (called "reps") for each exercise, twice a week. That meant I was lifting the weights in each hand six times for each exercise.

After my armpits stopped shrieking from the new workout, I increased the program as follows:

Week 2:   2 sets of 8 reps of the 6 exercises; 3 times a week

Week 3:   3 sets of 8 reps of the 6 exercises; 3 times a week

At that point I returned to the sports store where I selected a set of 5-pound weight and started again with the same routine, but heavier weights.

The next step up was 8-pounds and then 10, then 12. There's no way I will become muscle woman at this rate, but that's fine with me. It's about becoming firm. It's about small beginnings.

You might be able to go at a faster pace; increasing the number of reps or the number of pounds you are lifting. Or you might need to start out with less weights or fewer reps. The point is to start. And make it work for you.

Jesus wants us to have a firm foundation of faith, too. And He doesn't expect this faith to come in giant leaps. He expects us to step out in faith and move forward, a little at a time. Faith sometimes *does* work in giant leaps. However, for most people, growth in our faith is more a matter of inching forward; becoming a little bit stronger every day. Faith is a lot like body building.

Additionally, as our personal faith strengthens, we help to collectively build up the body of Christ (His church) just as lifting weights helps build our overall physical body which is the temple of the Lord. Face it, girlfriends, strength training is a good thing, physically and spiritually.

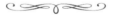

THINKING IT THROUGH: Have you ever lifted weights? If the idea is not pleasant to you, how can you make it pleasant? Can you turn on music and pump those muscles to the beat? Can you exercise while you're doing something you enjoy, like watching a movie? Can you invite a girlfriend, husband or child to join you and laugh while you're doing it so as to muffle the grunts? Do you think you're too weak to even begin? What *can* you lift? This book? Start where you are.

PRAYER: Heavenly Father, help me be strong for you. As I work on my muscles, please work on my most important muscle, my heart. Jesus, help me remember that I can do all things through you, because you strengthen me—even doing types of physical things that feel hard or unwomanly to me at first. Inspire in me, Holy Spirit, a desire to be strong for you. Amen.

SMALL BEGINNINGS
Where do you need to begin a strength building program? What do you have you could lift? To how many reps will you commit?

Chapter 16

Mold Me; Shape Me

Yet, O LORD, you are our Father. We are the clay, you are the potter; we are all the work of your hand (Isaiah 64:8).

Every mother has one. It's made from red clay, sits on a wobbly bottom, and is formed by dips and mounds where 5-year old fingers pushed and squeezed to turn the flat piece of clay into a bowl. My mother's bowl also has a crack down one side and would disintegrate into mush if it ever got wet.

Grammar school bowls weren't much better; evidently not even good enough for Mom to keep. Or perhaps they *did* disintegrate into mush. Finally, I spent a year in high school trying to master a potter's wheel. Mom has one of those bowls too. Frankly it's not much better than the kindergarten one. It also is lopsided with a wobbly bottom but instead of my little fingerprints, it's covered with spirals made by my hands as the clay spun beneath them on the wheel. This bowl has been painted and fired so it is less likely to turn to mush. Still Mom is evidently taking no chances. The bowl contains nothing more substantial than paperclips. The small ones.

Mold Me; Shape Me

When I think about Scripture and my personal experience with clay, I realize how hard it is to make something good out of something wet and mushy. Spiritually, when we try to make ourselves into pots, they turn out lopsided with wobbly bottoms and are not useful for even something so insubstantial as paperclips. Fortunately, God is a master potter and when we let Him mold and shape our lumpy clay, we become a masterpiece.

But maybe we're not letting God finish his masterpiece when it comes to our bodies. Are we spiritually moldable but physically inflexible? We can work on being spiritually moldable by spending time with God. We can work on being physically moldable by training our muscles, joints, and tendons to flex and stretch.

Especially as we age, everything seems to tighten up. But not in a good way. The muscles attached to the tendons no longer want to stretch and move with the same range of motion we used to have. One of the best things we can do to look and feel younger then, may be to work our muscles, so we don't moan every time we move.

I like to remember the dancing days of my youth. I envision myself as the ballerina I never was. Maybe I never ended up on stage with the American Ballet Theatre, but I can spend a few moments with them inside my brain, stretching and kicking, plie-ing and pointing my dainty little size 9-1/2 wide tootsies.

I know I need to move and be strong and I know I also need to be flexible. Physically what can I do? Forget trying to touch my toes. I know they're down there and I can even see them if I suck in my belly. The question then is: what can I do?

Can I bend over and let my arms hang down; letting the weight of them pull my upper body toward the floor, thus stretching my neck, spine, hips and legs? Sure, I can do that, and I can even stand back up.

I can lean forward on one leg, bend my front knee and stretch the calves of my back leg. That even feels good! I can reach up toward the ceiling and imagine I'm touching heaven.

As long as we're imagining, let's put on some classical music and imagine we're dancing. We might even move a bit—maybe a ballet stretch or two. 'Ain't we just the most graceful?

Maybe not, but Jesus loves us anyway. He's right there in the front row holding a bouquet of roses ready to place in our arms at the end of our performance, as we gracefully slide into a curtsey at the final curtain fall.

We can put those roses in our lovely ceramic vase. Not the one with the wobbly bottom. No, the one Jesus is making when he molds us with His hands. The beautiful, strong, firm vase that is flexible both spiritually and physically.

THINKING IT THROUGH: Are you currently doing any form of flexibility exercise? What are you capable of doing today? What would you like to be doing in a few weeks or months? You may not be quite ready to enroll in an advanced yoga or tai chi class, but you can first plan one or two flexibility exercises you are willing to start with and increase the number of reps you will be doing over a period of time. Start slow and easy. You may be sore. That just means you're working those tired muscles, ligaments, and tendons. That's a good thing.

PRAYER: Heavenly Father, make me moldable to your will. Holy Spirit help me become more flexible physically too so I can move more freely about this world and be your hands and feet. Jesus, thank you for your precious nail-pierced hands and feet and for the salvation they bought for me. Amen.

SMALL BEGINNINGS
What three stretching exercises can you do?
Set a goal of 4 or 8 reps for each to do today
and three more times this week.

Chapter 17

Now I Lay Me Down to Sleep

I will lie down and sleep in peace, for you alone, O Lord, make me dwell in safety (Psalm 4:8).

When my kids were little, I made up a bedtime story about the Midnight Repairmen. In my story, the friendly, hard-working Midnight Repairmen would come in the middle of the night and fix up our bodies while we slept. If my child got an owie during the day, Mom could paste on a band-aide and top it off with a kiss, but it was the Midnight Repairmen who did the real work of healing. In the morning, the owie was always much better.

Biologically, we know that our bodies need rest so we can recover our muscles, not over-tax our organs, and be prepared to work hard the next day. We also know that our white blood cells are the real repairmen. They march over to the site of an infection, eat away all the bad noogies and allow an owie to heal. Those white blood cells work hardest when we are in the very deepest cycle of sleep.

What this science means is that our bodies heal best not just when we're sleeping, but specifically during one part of our sleeping time.

By extension, if we aren't sleeping enough, we may not ever get into that deepest sleep cycle or may not stay in it long enough for God's Midnight Repairmen to do their stuff. Those owies stay owies longer. Our bodies break down and stay down. In short, we're telling our Midnight Repairmen they are laid off. How can we rebuild our temple when part of our reconstruction crew has hit the road?

We need rest. God knows that. In fact, He told us so on day seven by His example. Rest is sacred.

How is your sleep? Do you get the recommended eight hours? If not, why not? What is preventing you from getting eight hours and what can you do to change that? Do you need more than eight hours? It's not a sin to admit that. It doesn't even mean you're defective. You need what you need. You should know what you need and strive for that amount.

If you're allowing adequate time for sleep but not feeling rested, what is preventing that? Do you need white noise from a fan to cover up external noises that may be waking you at night? Is your bed or pillow comfortable? Is your room too hot or too cold? Are you consuming caffeine too late in the day? Are you eating too much or the wrong type of food too late in the evening so that you have a higher blood sugar level or acid reflux?

Are you focused on worries or stresses so that your mind prevents you from falling asleep quickly? Are you getting enough exercise, so your body naturally seeks relaxation? Could you be suffering from sleep apnea where your throat closes many times during the night not allowing you sufficient oxygen and taking you out of deep sleep?

It's time for you to look seriously at your sleep and find out what is preventing you from getting the best sleep you can get. Then take steps to make your sleep better. Become an expert on your own temple.

One thing I have learned is that every time I have trouble falling asleep, it is usually because I have forgotten to end my day in prayer. If I pray and still can't sleep, then I get back into prayer. I keep laying my worries at Jesus' feet until I'm no longer carrying them myself. Do I then fall asleep because of something Jesus did in answer to my prayer? Maybe. Probably even.

There's also science behind ending your day in prayer.

Waves are everywhere in nature. God created sound waves, light waves, and ocean waves. Even when there's an earthquake, the ground rolls in waves.

On a smaller scale, God made our brains emit different types of waves, too. You have heard about them. There are gamma brain waves, beta brain waves, alpha brain waves, and theta brain waves. These different types of brain waves can be observed and measured by scientific equipment.

When we are in prayer or meditation, our brains emit theta waves. Coincidently, theta waves are the same type of wave our brains emit *when we first fall asleep*. From early sleep, we then can move into deep sleep, during which our brains emit delta waves. That's when those Midnight Repairmen come out and do their thing.

Let's look at how what *we* first do takes us toward what *God* can do:

- Pray (*We* cause theta waves to be produced through our conscious effort) →

- That takes us into sleep (our brain keeps producing theta waves without us doing anything consciously) →

- Our sleep deepens and ultimately emits delta waves (nature's progression into healing sleep).

- God's miracle of how our bodies operate sends out the Midnight Repairmen to help rebuild our temple.

This theta wave connection suggests that if we place ourselves into a theta wave state by praying, we are that much closer to drifting naturally from prayer to sleep.

Have you ever fallen asleep while you're praying? Me too. And I don't think God is a bit annoyed when we do that. Wouldn't you be pleased if your children fell asleep pouring their hearts out to you?

God understands our need for rest. He works while we sleep and has created tiny miracle repairmen to work inside our bodies to rebuild our temples even when we aren't doing anything to make it happen. But we can make God's work easier and start sooner if we place our brains into theta waves first through prayer.

Try ending your day with God. He doesn't sleep. But we can, knowing He's making sure the earth keeps spinning and the stars don't crash into each other. And He's right there cradling us in His arms and singing us His sweet lullaby.

> *The Lord your God is with you, the Mighty Warrior who saves. He will take great delight in you; in his love he will no longer rebuke you, but will rejoice over you with singing* (Zephaniah 3:17).

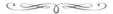

THINKING IT THROUGH: How many hours of sleep a night do you need? Do you feel rested when you get them? Take a look at your sleep and your sleeping situation. What can you do to make it better?

PRAYER: Heavenly Father, thank you for this day and for walking with me through it. I know I did not do everything perfectly today. But I know you rejoiced with me when I did things to rebuild your temple and know you forgive me when I fall short.

Make clear to me one lesson I learned today, Holy Spirit, about how my body works, what it needs or how to rebuild it. Set that lesson into my consciousness and help me do better tomorrow. Amen

---

SMALL BEGINNINGS
What is the biggest sleep issue you have?
What might be the cause of it?
What can you do today to help resolve that issue?

Part V

What Else Goes in the Temple?

Chapter 18

Cleanse Me, Oh Lord

"Everyone who drinks this water will be thirsty again, but whoever drinks the water I give him will never thirst. Indeed, the water I give him will become in him a spring of water welling up to eternal life" (John 4:13).

I love this passage. Jesus understands how much we thirst to know God. He understands that, like water, knowing God is essential to our spiritual survival. It also reminds us that without Jesus, we have no chance at eternal life with God. It is through Jesus' living water (salvation through His sacrifice) that we gain access to eternal communion with God.

Although we recognize that this Scripture refers to spiritual springs of water, let's apply the Scripture literally for a moment. When God made our physical bodies, He made them to be 60-70% water. Think about it, girlfriend. If Jesus in human form was 70% water, he was not only spiritual "living water," he was physically "living water" as well.

And we were made in His physical image.

Our physical bodies must have physical water to survive. We can last five weeks without eating (theoretically) but we can only last three days without water. Three days? How biblical!

But we need more than just to drink water. It needs to be good water. Throughout history sailors died at sea because they didn't have adequate fresh water to drink. All that water in the ocean wasn't drinkable. It only caused them to die faster if they drank it.

Today we are warned that if there is an emergency, we should not drink water from the tap. Broken pipes and problems at the source could cause our running water to be contaminated, resulting in dysentery or other life-threatening problems. Instead, in an emergency, our water must be boiled, chlorinated or filtered. We need good water for good life.

Let's think about what we drink. Our bodies naturally crave fluids and tell us we need those fluids by making us feel thirsty. But often we drink anything and everything *but* water to quench our thirst. We drink soda, coffee, juice, sweetened tea. But where's the water? It's not just fluid we need. It's pure, clear water.

One of the things water does is cleanse our bodies. It flushes toxins out of our bodies. It washes us clean from the inside out. God wants to cleanse us spiritually. And He also intended us to be cleansed physically inside as well. Good, clean water is one way God intends to do this.

But there is another way as well. Look at Matthew 15:16-20:

> *"Are you still so dull?" Jesus asked them. "Don't you see that whatever enters the mouth goes into the stomach and then out of the body?"*

It's not just what goes into the body (food) but what comes out that is important. Here Scripture was showing that we shouldn't focus on the particulars of what we eat or how we eat them as much as what we say.

But taken literally, this verse recognizes that God created our physical bodies to rid ourselves of waste products. Need I spell it out for you? We need to regulate our innards. We need to poop, gals.

Are we doing things to clog up the works? Are we eating too much processed food and heavy proteins that are hard for our bodies to digest? Are we flushing our bodies with enough life-giving water? Are we getting enough fresh fruits and vegetables that contain cleansing fiber?

If your house had a gas leak, you wouldn't close all the windows to keep the gas trapped inside. You'd open the doors and windows (after turning off the gas) to get the toxic gases out. Your body needs to do the same thing—remove the toxic substances—so we can continue to function.

Just like God goes about cleansing us spiritually, so do we need to cleanse our bodies by making sure the toxins, residue, and waste are flushed from the cells so our machines can function properly. These bodies are the temples of the Lord. You wouldn't go to church and bring along your kitchen garbage, dump it on the altar, and leave. So too do we need to make sure our temples of the Lord are cleansed internally.

Our bodies are cleansed internally both by drinking water and by consuming adequate amounts of fiber. God has provided adequate fiber in living plants for us to eat. But if we eat too much processed food or not enough fresh fruit, veggies, and whole grains, we may not be getting enough fiber.

As we work our plan and take it step by step to a healthier living, we may need to supplement our fiber intake initially. Then slowly we may be able to step away from fiber supplements until we are providing our bodies with enough of God's food and pure water that will cleanse us from the inside out.

You know the nutritional advice that you should get at least 25 grams of fiber a day. Are you? Do you eat at least 5 servings of fruit and veggies a day and make sure your bread is 100% whole grains? Do you need to supplement your diet with fiber?

There are all kinds of edible sources of fiber available now that are quite delicious and can be incorporated into your overall meal plan. If you want to work on getting your extra fiber at the same time as your water, you can drink flavored fiber-enhanced water. If you don't like the taste of high fiber food or fiber-enhanced water, or want to use your calories elsewhere, then there are zero calorie fiber supplements in pill or chewable form. In other words, there are no more excuses for not getting your fiber.

God created us to work perfectly. Put in the good stuff and get rid of the waste. God not only wants a strong temple; He also wants a clean one.

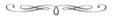

THINKING IT THROUGH: The medical community says we should drink at least eight cups of water a day and consume 25 grams of fiber. Are you? If not, what can you do? Can you set a timer and drink a glass of water every hour? Can you increase your water by first drinking more low-calorie juices and watering them down over several days, so you are drinking more water over time and less "drink"? Or can you add fresh lemon to your water so that it becomes a treat? Can you increase the number of fresh fruits or veggies you eat each day? Can you switch your white bread with white fiber bread this week and then switch to double fiber whole grain bread next week?

PRAYER: Heavenly Father, help me strive to be godly in all areas of my life, including when it comes to cleansing my physical body. Holy Spirit remind me today to drink water and eat fiber in sufficient amounts so my body can do the miracle of cleansing you intended. Thank you, Jesus, for being the living water we need to quench our spiritual thirst and for the eternal life that comes through you. Amen.

SMALL BEGINNINGS
Do you drink enough liquid?
Do you get adequate fiber in your diet?
What can you do today to increase liquid and fiber?

Chapter 19

Vitamins, Supplements, Medications

But the Lord provided a great fish to swallow Jonah, and Jonah was inside the fish three days and three nights (Jonah 1:17).

I had been taking omega 3 fish oil capsules for several years but decided to stop taking them because in my never planned out, haphazard attempt to cut calories, I decided I'd skip the supplement and save the calories.

Now that I was developing an actual plan this time, I decided to include fish oil supplements. It became a matter of allocating some of my daily calories for a supplement that I felt improved my health. One morning I opened the jar and stared at the glistening jelly capsules trying to decide how many to take. Well, I could take two, I guess. But four was the recommended dosage. What would that mean in terms of calories?

I turned the bottle around and there in bold black letters it said 35 calories per serving. I gulped, trying to do the math. One hundred forty calories. Oh, well. I was committed. I shook out four capsules and then some other bold black letters caught my eyeballs.

One serving was four capsules. That's 35 calories *for all four capsules*. I'd been worrying about something that wasn't even true. And God tells us not to do that. Omega 3 is now on my list of daily supplements.

Are there supplements you should be taking but don't? Maybe because of a silly reason like mine? Here are a few silly excuses I've heard (or said).

- My calcium pills are too big. Solution: spend $3 for a pill cutter and take two small halves instead of one big one. Or get the delicious chewy ones instead.

- My multi vitamins make me queasy. Solution: find a multi that contains no B vitamins and then get a sublingual Vitamin B that bypasses your stomach.

- Aspirin is harsh on my stomach. Or it dissolves in my throat. Solution: try a baby aspirin. They are gentler and taste better if they accidently dissolve before going all the way down.

- Fish oil makes me burp. Solution: try kelp oil instead (unless you are allergic to shellfish). No burping. Or take the fish oil just before bedtime. You won't jostle your body around, causing so many burps.

- Supplements are expensive. Solution: You don't need to buy only high-profile name brands of vitamins and supplements. Do your research; read bottle labels and buy generic. Better yet, buy generic when they are on sale!

What can you do to encourage yourself to take the supplements and medications you need to take?

Every day an expert comes out claiming there's one more supplement we must take in order to live healthy, longer, better lives. That's between you and your health care provider. This chapter is about encouraging you to take the vitamins, supplements, and prescribed medications you need, to take them when you're supposed to, and to take them in the amounts prescribed.

Women over 40 wrestle with many painful and annoying physical and emotional consequences of hormonal changes. The hormonal levels we were used to for the last several decades seem to have vaporized and we are suddenly running our hormone tank on fumes. Dealing with hormonal changes is a huge part of our health at this age.

Determining the need for and then the level and type of hormone replacement can be a long and arduous process. Each woman is unique and what works well for one of us may cause the rest of us to shriek or collapse in a heap of sobbing mush. Today though there are many types of relief, from all-out chemical hormone replacement to bio identical, topical creams and gels, to a recommendation to simply adjust what we eat. Because hormones are so tricky and yet have such a pronounced effect on our overall health and feeling of well-being, getting relief and getting it right is worth the effort.

Addressing the issue of hormone replacement or other treatment, needs to be undertaken in conjunction with a professional who knows your body. Do not be unduly afraid of the process. Our baby-boomer generation is the largest population of women who are near or have reached menopause. Therefore medicine, science, and homeopathy are now paying more attention to our changing needs. And providing relief.

Throughout everything we address in this chapter, as it applies to vitamins, supplements, and prescription medications, it is important to take them as we should. An added benefit of taking all those tablets is that you'll have to drink more water. Less to nag you about later.

After all, if the whale could swallow Jonah, I can take a few pills.

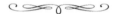

THINKING IT THROUGH: Are you resisting taking vitamins, minerals or supplements? Consider picking two or three supplements you'll commit to and then take them. You don't need to take one of everything out there. Or maybe this month, you'll commit to just taking a multi vitamin and add a vitamin D next month and omega 3 the month after that. Work your way into it. Do your research, ask your doctor, and determine what works for *your* temple.

PRAYER: Heavenly Father, thank you for the minds you have given us. Thank you for the people who understand the workings of our physical bodies and who can recommend resources from your world to help me rebuild my temple. Help me, Holy Spirit to take the vitamins, supplements, and medicines I need each day to strengthen and repair my temple. Thank you, Jesus that faith in you is what gives me spiritual health. Amen.

SMALL BEGINNINGS
What prescription, over the counter medications,
and supplements do you take? Which are necessary?
What might be missing? Talk with your doctor
and decide which ones to take. Then, take them.

Part VI

Miscellaneous

Chapter 20

Traveling

Whatever city you enter, and they receive you, eat such things as are set before you. And heal the sick there, and say to them, 'The kingdom of God has come near to you' (Luke 10:8-9).

I hate to travel. Let me sleep in my great bed. Leave me here with my drawers and cupboards holding everything I need. You go on ahead. I'll just hang out here where I have a routine and know how to use it.

One of the things that's difficult for me when traveling is getting out of my routine. I struggle to exercise while I'm gone, and any sort of rational eating plan ends up in the lost luggage section of my life. Chances are that a trip out of town means I have to start my routine all over again when I get home. And we all know that one of the hardest parts of living a healthy lifestyle is getting started. Or getting started again.

Even if you love to travel, chances are you face the same difficulties. Maybe you use the traveling as an excuse to fall off your plan. It's okay to admit it. This is about our journey to recognizing our struggles and finding ways to get through or around them.

So, let's just start with the premise that travel usually means a break in our routine and a challenge to continue the progress we've made rebuilding our temple. Even if you don't have a trip looming in your future, now is a great time to plan for when you do.

Let's break down Luke 10:8-9 set out at the beginning of this chapter. These are the instructions Jesus gave His disciples when He sent them out.

- Enter the city
- Allow people to receive you
- Eat what's set in front of you
- Heal the sick
- Speak the gospel

How can we relate this Scripture to rebuilding our temple?

Enter the city. For us, this means we need to become familiar with where we are going. If you are heading to Chicago in January, chances are you won't be able to get out for a leisurely walk through the countryside. In fact, probably you will have to settle for some sort of indoor exercise.

You also need to know whether you are staying at a hotel or a home. What types of activities will be available? If the hotel has no gym, can you take any form of exercise equipment with you, such as a jump rope or stretch bands? Or can you bring an exercise DVD to play on your computer? Or can you plan a simple routine of exercises that does not require equipment so that at least you stay true to a commitment to exercising in some form?

If the weather allows, is there a park or nature walk nearby that could entice you? If there is no park, can you plan a walking route you could take near your hotel and print out a map while you're still at home? You may not actually need a map, but any pre-planning and effort you make beforehand, may encourage you to get out and exercise once you're there.

If you absolutely cannot figure out how to incorporate exercise into your trip, can you at least make sure you have not taken any days off of exercise for the several-day period before your trip and make sure you exercise on the first day back? But really, is there any excuse for not at least stretching? That is exercise, too.

In other words, we can apply this first part of Jesus' instructions. We can learn all we can about the city we will enter so we can create a plan to keep working on our rebuilding while we are away from home.

Allow people to receive you. What is the purpose of your travel? Are you traveling for business? If so, think how you can grow business relationships on your trip. When focusing on the relationships you won't have as much time alone where you may be tempted to eat out of feelings of boredom or loneliness. If you are traveling with a female co-worker, invite her to join you at the gym or for a walk. Working together (or working out together) is an ideal way to build relationships along with muscles.

If you are traveling with friends and family, do the same—focus on relationships. Make the trip about the people rather than the food and drink. Encourage those you love to rebuild their temples by joining you in moving those muscles.

Eat what is in front of you. Here's that pesky third instruction you're waiting to snag and run off to the bakery with. Sorry, but Jesus didn't tell His disciples to eat whatever they saw plus what was baking in the brick oven, what was still growing in the fields, and everything packed on the back of the camel sitting out front. Our application is to not eat what's stored in the hotel mini fridge and everything stacked at the convenience store checkout. Nor does it even mean to necessarily eat *everything* and *all* of what is in front of you.

This instruction is more about being gracious; about not asking for special treatment, and about being amiable. I like to think of it as Jesus' way of encouraging us to focus on the people we are with as opposed to the food itself.

A modern way we can apply this instruction has to do with planning. If you are running from airplane to airplane or driving 10 hours a day, you may find your eating schedule has gone haywire. When you are able to grab a meal, you may be so ravenous that you overeat or make poor choices.

Instead, you can plan ahead for that possibility. You can take along items to snack on to avoid becoming ravenous during travel times. You can plan emergency snacks while still at home. And try them out. Are they foods you enjoy eating (while still being nutritious) that you will choose to eat while away from home? It won't do any good to bring wholesome snacks if you won't actually eat them.

If you will be eating at restaurants, can you determine ahead of time what restaurants are available in the area where you will be staying? You may be able to download menus from those restaurants on the computer and plan ahead what you will order. When you arrive at the restaurant, you won't even have to crack open the menu. You will already know what to order. The waiter will place that food in front of you. Eat it.

If you are visiting family or friends, you can let them know ahead of time that you are trying to eat a healthful way. You can ask their help in doing what you need to do to become a healthier person, without asking for too much special treatment. If your request is too difficult though, simply focus on the fellowship rather than the food, remembering Jesus' instruction to eat what is in front of you. Turn your focus on eating what is in front of you, but maybe not all of it.

Taken another way, by planning ahead for what you will eat, "the what" will not be in the back of your mind. Rather, "the what" will be in the front of your mind. So, following Jesus' instruction, eat what is in front of you.

Heal the sick. This instruction applies to you. It is your temple you are trying to rebuild. It is your body that needs healing. As disciples, Jesus admonishes us to heal the sick. So, when these bodies that need healing are traveling, we need to do our best to heal them. We can keep this instruction in our heads and in our hearts. We can focus on continuing to do the things we need to do to heal ourselves even while we are away from home.

Speak the gospel. We should do this anyway. But what does it have to do with rebuilding the temple? Two things. First, we are not the only ones who need rebuilding. Rebuilding for some people may also have to do with spiritual rebuilding. So, we can speak the gospel. We can share it with others so they can rebuild their temple spiritually. And as you speak the gospel loudly and with courage, it will encourage you by being instilled deeper in your own heart.

Second, when you are speaking, you are not eating. Have you noticed how so many thin people are the biggest chatterboxes at the table? They take simply forever to finish their meal. They're the ones who don't take seconds because dinner time has come and gone, and everyone is waiting for them to finish.

Also, we are told that longer it takes you to finish a meal, the longer your brain has to receive the signal from the stomach that you are full. Use thin, chatty people as your role models. And as long as you're speaking, you may as well speak the gospel.

My friend Becki has learned a lot about how to manage health issues while traveling. This is what she had to say:

> *As a frequent traveler, I can certainly relate to this chapter! It used to be that staying in a hotel meant junk food snacking for Alan and I both. We would go to a local grocery or the gift shop and load up....M&M's, ice cream, chips...you name it! I didn't eat like that at home, but traveling always meant I was on vacation (even if Alan was working) and when you're on vacation, anything goes, right?*
>
> *When I decided I just couldn't do that anymore, it was harder than I thought it would be. I usually have my bars with me now and if I can get to a grocery store, I get grapes and apples. The problem was that I was so conditioned to eating junk food; I craved it whenever we got into a hotel room.*
>
> *I'm not very good at using the exercise rooms at hotels. Now if I'm tagging along on a business trip, I look up places to go explore in the area. I love finding parks and nature preserves to walk around in if the weather permits. I also like museums and, of course, antique malls! I try to walk as much as possible.*

Becki has learned how to successfully continue doing what she needs to do to stay healthy even when she is away from home. We can learn to do it, too.

Our Heavenly Father made this world and then Jesus told us to go out into it. Home may be where our heart is, but Jesus' heart is in the world. Like everything we want to accomplish, sometimes facing challenges of sticking with healthy lifestyle choices requires planning. We don't have to fear that part of travel. Instead, we can plan and do our best.

THINKING IT THROUGH: What exercise can you do when you travel? If you can't do your regular routine, what can you substitute, making sure the substitute exercises are similar enough or use the same muscles used in your regular exercise. If they are totally different, consider beginning those exercises several days before your trip so your muscles get used to moving that way before you leave. You don't want to spend your travel time with sore muscles and you also don't want to set your program back by not exercising.

You will feel like your trip was a success, regardless of what else happened, if you return having made good food choices, gotten some exercise in, and followed your other plans, including taking your vitamins, supplements, medications, water, and fiber. New circumstances make it easy to get our routines off track. Your body needs to be kept in an even state of nutrition and hydration. It's too easy to develop constipation and diarrhea as it is without making those problems worse by what we put or don't put into our bodies.

PRAYER: Heavenly Father, thank you for the opportunities to move through your world and experience other places and people. Jesus, I know that your heart is in this world and that you want me to go out into it. Holy Spirit, I ask for your guidance in continuing to work toward better health even when I am away from my home and routine, where I may be more easily tempted to make unhealthy choices. Amen.

SMALL BEGINNINGS
What travel plans do you have coming up?
How does Luke speak to you about preparing
a healthy mindset for traveling? What one thing
will you focus on from Luke for your next trip?

Chapter 21

Seeing Your Beauty

Your beauty should not come from outward adornment, such as braided hair and the wearing of gold jewelry and fine clothes. Instead, it should be that of your inner self, the unfading beauty of a gentle and quiet spirit, which is of great worth in God's sight. For this is the way the holy women of the past who put their hope in God used to make themselves beautiful (1 Peter 3:3-5).

God loves a gentle and quiet spirit. For some Christian women though it's hard to set aside a desire to be physically beautiful and focus only on spiritual beauty. Let's face it, girls. We want to also be physically beautiful.

God gave us that desire to be beautiful both spiritually *and* physically. Fortunately, even if our temple is presently in disrepair, it is still beautiful.

Sometimes it's hard to see our own beauty. We may feel so horribly fat or weak or sick that we can only see what we've done to our physical selves or how our temples are broken. But God made us beautiful. And we still *are* beautiful—yes, even now!

Maybe we should set aside the 360-degree mirror for a moment. Some of us aren't ready to look at ourselves dispassionately and actually see the beauty that is standing in front of us. Instead, it might be more helpful right now to use a small hand mirror to focus on the parts right now instead of the whole. Maybe we need to glimpse one tiny bit of our body that we will agree is beautiful, even now.

Run your fingers through your hair. Feel its silkiness. Imagine the hair follicles underneath your skin, cells growing and dividing, creating longer, brand-new, fresh hair for tomorrow. Think about a breeze blowing through your hair. Imagine the feel of it tickling your forehead. Tuck it behind your ear. Does a tiny bit of it curl back around your ear to caress your cheek? If it is long, let it flow down your neck. Imagine it is a silken scarf.

Look closely at your face. Take in each of your features in turn. Notice your forehead. Is it tall? Wide? Narrow? Your eyebrows— are they high? Arched? Thick? Thin? What color are the hairs? Wonder at the way God gave us eyebrows to shelter our eyes from particles. Smile at the way God gave us the ability to use our eyebrows to express emotion. Lift them high in surprise. Squish them together in puzzlement. Smile wide and notice what they do.

Look at your eyes. Get close to a mirror and really look at them. Notice their shape and how God placed them on your face. Are they far apart or close together? Notice that God placed them in the center of your face horizontally and right above the bridge of your nose, just perfectly located to hold your glasses!

Stare into your eyes. Notice the tiny blood vessels in the white rushing nutrients into your eyeballs to enable you to see. Notice the dark pupils and think about how God made the miracle of an iris that can open wide when it is dark and close in protection in bright light. Notice the color and visual texture of your pupils. Did you think your eyes were just brown or blue or green? Notice the variation of colors that exist in your eyes that make them uniquely yours.

Look at the bones of your face and the shape of it. Is your face roundish, square, oval, heart shaped, triangular? What about your nose? Look at its function and think about all it does for you. How it makes your life better. How often do we pick a shampoo, hand lotion or body wash because of the smell? Praise God for your nose, for its function, for what it does, and for how it makes your body whole.

Look at your lips—their shape and size. Are your lips full or thin? Is your mouth small or large? What is the shape of your mouth? Notice the tiny vertical creases in your lips. No, not the ones from sun damage or age. The ones God even gave to newborn babies. They're like an accordion, allowing your mouth to stretch wide when you need to and then spring back into place when your mouth is closed. That way you don't have great big droopy lips all the time or scream in pain when you smile and need the skin to stretch. Praise God for that!

Take yourself through every part of your body. Look at its shape and function and praise God for it. Every woman has a part of their body they like. Even you. For me it's my eyes. I also happen to think I have beautiful feet, too. Even if they are size 9-1/2 wide.

Pick a part of your body that you like and really appreciate it. Notice what it looks like. What it feels like. What is its function?

If you think your hands are your best feature, move them. Watch how your fingers flex and bend. Really appreciate them for the marvelous creation they are. Clap them and lift them in praise to God.

Each and every part of your body is like that—a marvelous creation and beautiful in its individuality. And even better in unison with the rest.

> *Just as each of us has one body with many members and these members do not all have the same function, so in Christ we who are many form one body, and each member belongs to all the others* (Romans 12:4-5).

Paul reminds us that each part of our body is part of the whole. And each of us is part of the body of Christ. Christ wants our physical bodies to be the best they can be because He created them. So, love them as He does.

What does this Scripture have to do with health? For one thing, it reminds us of the miracle God created when He created us. It reminds us that He has done His part in building our temple and that it's our part to rebuild and maintain it. It reminds us that our body is a wonderful thing of beauty and worth taking care of.

So, focus on the beauty of your body. Then do one thing today and every day to feel the beauty. Put on perfume and fully experience the joy of the scent. Close your eyes and inhale. Understand the beauty of the fragrance and how it has now become a part of your body.

Or spend an extra three minutes on your hair. Put it up or down or curl it or stick a flower behind one ear. Enjoy the feel and the flow of your hair.

Or put on lipstick or lip-gloss even if you never ever wear it. Just for the fun and the beauty of it. Notice how it glides across your lips. Line your lips with the lipstick and notice how God formed your lips like no one else's lips in the world. Notice how the upper lip forms a butterfly's wings; how the bottom lip is fuller than the top and how the two meet perfectly at the edges and in the center; how they become fuller or almost disappear when you smile, to reveal your teeth beneath. Smile and know that God is smiling too because He made you and you are beautiful.

You may also want to spend time relaxing and meditating on how God created such a beautiful miracle when He created you. Form a vision of yourself in your head. It's okay to make the vision the one you are working to achieve. It might be God's vision, too. Focus on the vision; make it real. Make it something to help you stay focused on what you are doing.

All of us women want to be beautiful. Remember that you already are.

THINKING IT THROUGH: What part of your body do you think is your best feature? Look at each of your body parts and really think about them and their function. Marvel at God's wisdom in creating them as part of the whole. Imagine how your body would function (or not function) without them. Focus on gratitude for the beauty God sees when He looks at you.

PRAYER: Heavenly Father, thank you for the beauty you created in this world. Thank you for making me beautiful, too. Jesus, point out some part of my physical body that is especially beautiful. Holy Spirit remind me throughout the day how I can rebuild this temple to regain and maintain its beauty for God. Amen.

SMALL BEGINNINGS
What is one of your best physical features?
How can you focus on your beauty to encourage
you as you seek better health?

Chapter 22

When You Fast

"When you fast, put oil on your head and wash your face, so that it will not be obvious to men that you are fasting, but only to your Father, who is unseen; and your Father, who sees what is done in secret, will reward you" (Matthew 6:17-18).

Jesus fasted for 40 days and 40 nights. Other Old Testament heroes fasted, too as did New Testament heroes. People pray and fast all the time—even today. What does it mean? *Why* do they do it? *How* do they do it? Should we do it, too?

Bible heroes prayed and fasted when there was something important at stake. When there was a decision to be made. When there was a battle to be fought. Whenever the strength of God was especially needed.

The how's are less clear. Fast and pray. And do it quietly and look good while you're doing it. That's all the Bible tells us. Does it mean no food and no water? Does it mean water is okay? If water, what about juice? Or broth? Could we really fast without food?

When You Fast

Should we? Does a fast mean simply no eating during daylight hours? Or giving up a specific food?

There's no way that I—a non-medically-degreed layperson—is going to recommend that you include a day without eating as part of your plan. You have personal health issues. Your blood sugar may not be stable enough to handle a no-food day. So, let's stop right here and ask why I have a chapter about prayer and fasting.

For me, prayer and fasting are about submitting my will to God's. We may not be able (yet) to submit our will to God's in all things, every day. But perhaps we can submit one thing to God for one day while praying and seeking His guidance for something larger than that one thing we are giving up.

Maybe then, fasting might be creating a day of prayer and giving up one thing which most stifles your health and crumbles your temple. If you struggle with simple carbohydrates, could you give up foods that combine white flour and white sugar? For one day?

What would that look like? It might mean that you give up your morning donut and substitute it with a slice of whole grain toast and a dab of low-fat peanut butter.

Could you do one day of prayer and that type of fasting to submit your will to God's?

If you eat too much animal fat, could you give up meat for one day, while eating more vegetables and eggs or cheese for protein?

Could you do one day of prayer and that type of fasting to submit your will to God's?

If you struggle with too much caffeine, could you spend one day drinking a coffee blended from regular coffee and decaf?

Could you do one day of prayer and that type of fasting to submit your will to God's? And then drink only decaf on your next fast?

Wait a minute. Rewind. What does she mean "on your next fast?"

What I mean is that you might consider fasting on a regular basis. Not a no-food fast. But a fast to surrender one part of your physical temple to God. One day a week; one day a month; or one day a year. One day at a time. One day.

A small beginning.

Fasting is not a sacrifice in exchange for a blessing. Rather, fasting is going without something in order to focus on something more important. It is denying the desire of our flesh in order to move into deeper faith. Remember that the Holy Spirit lives in us. When we deny the flesh part of our bodies, we give greater power to the Spirit in us. We are then able to move into deeper communion with God through prayer.

There are numerous Scriptures related to fasting. So many, in fact, that it is impossible to ignore the suggestion that fasting maybe should be a part of every Christian's walk. Here are verses that describe reasons why we should fast:

- We should fast to honor God (Matthew 5:6; 6:16-18, Luke 2:37; Acts 13:2)

- We should fast to humble ourselves (2 Chronicles 7:14-15)

- We should fast to obtain healing (Isaiah 59:1-2; 1 Corinthians 11:30; James 5:13-18)

- We should fast to receive deliverance from bondage (Isaiah 58: 6-9; Matthew 17:21)

- We should fast for God's will to be revealed (Daniel 9:3, 9: 20-21; 10:2-13)

- We should fast for revival of our faith (Acts 1:4; 14; 2:16-21; Joel 2:12-18)

- We should fast for repentance (Jeremiah 29:11-14; James 4:8-10)

Any of these would be good enough reason to fast. I personally like the first one: to honor God.

What about the first part of the phrase "prayer and fasting" then? What do we pray about?

We pray about whatever is the focus for the fast. Is it prayer for a specific concern? A specific person? A specific trouble? Or a focus for the world at large? Do you pray for every possible thing you can think of?

For us, we might focus our prayer on one specific aspect of our health—overcoming cravings, making wrong food choices, a health threat looming or one we are currently going through. Plan ahead the subject of your prayer. Or simply open your prayer to the leading of the Holy Spirit.

How do you structure your praying? If you have a whole day available, are you able to spend the day in prayer, reading Scripture and meditating—with adequate concentration? What fits your lifestyle? Your personality? Your need?

If you doubt you'd not be able to fast for a whole day, here's something to consider: If you regularly stop eating at 7:00 pm and have breakfast at 7:00 am, that means you are going without food for 12 hours. That's one-half of a 24-hour day. Essentially you are regularly doing a one-half day fast every day. If you plan to fast for a full day, you're already half-way done before you even begin.

You may ultimately decide to create a permanent fast—wholly giving up one specific food, drink, substance or practice. It is up to you and the Holy Spirit what your prayer and fasting will be like. Let the Spirit lead you.

THINKING IT THROUGH: What are you willing to sacrifice in terms of a fast? Can you give up all food for today? Or all solid food? Or all food just during daylight hours? What can you do, without causing your temple to crumble further?

How can you focus your prayer? Can you pray a simple prayer throughout the day, continuously? Or will you commit to praying every half hour, every hour or every 2 hours? Do you need to set a timer to remind yourself? Recognize that God is probably okay if you stumble or need prompts. Picture Jesus smiling every time your timer goes *beep*.

PRAYER: Father, Son, and Holy Spirit, help me focus today on rebuilding this temple for you. Guide me in my desire to offer a sacrifice to honor you. Amen.

SMALL BEGINNINGS
What one food or practice might you be willing to
give up to honor God?

Chapter 23

Have a Plan

What I have said, that will I bring about; what I have planned, that will I do (Isaiah 46:11).

What if God hadn't had a plan when he created creation? What if He'd just said, "I think I'll make some cuddly fur-covered creatures with pink toes"?

What if He'd then plopped them down in the middle of the water-covered earth? Those poor critters would have gasped, blinked up at God with their sad eyeballs, and slowly sank beneath the waves. Bye-bye, cuddly creatures.

Fortunately, that's not what God did. First God created the heavens and the earth as formless and empty. Kind of like us without God! From a human perspective, God created a blank canvas—a celestial white board upon which He could draw His plan in real-life.

What did God do next? He sent the Holy Spirit to hover over the water. I like to think of this as God's scouting party as if the Holy Spirit was sent to see what should be where and how and what it should all look like. An important first step in making a plan. Gather and evaluate the data.

What did God do next? He said, "Let there be light." Create light so you can see what you're doing.

God's plan went on to separate water from water and water from sky and days and nights. Then He created dry land and seas and vegetation. Then he set lights in the sky to serve as signs to mark seasons, days and years. In other words, God created time.

Only then did God create creatures—first in the water, then in the air, and finally on the land. Notice He didn't create any living creatures until He had already provided a specific place for them to live and food for them to consume.

Finally, God created us and gave us authority to rule over everything on earth. Once more, we are reminded that God created the place for us to live and the vegetation and critters for our needs before He created us. And even before day one at the beginning of creation, God already had an even bigger plan. Bigger than creating the entire universe? Yep. He created His plan for salvation through Jesus. He knew us that well.

God is the biggest planner ever. If we're created in His likeness then, we'll be better achievers if we, too, plan first. And the more detailed our plan, the more likely we will be to achieve it. God didn't just say, "Hey, let there be earth." He planned and took that plan one step at a time.

So, what's our plan? How should we go about rebuilding our temple?

Everyone has different issues they need to address. Perhaps you're not overweight; just under fit. Perhaps you're struggling with food allergies or food addictions. Maybe you need to follow a doctor's strict dietary regime. Maybe you're recovering from surgery or a health crisis. Maybe you have 100 pounds to lose or only three or all you know is that you need to change. What we need to do next then is plan.

Our plan, like the earth, may start out formless. But, like the Holy Spirit, we can hover and scout out where we are starting, where we need to go, and a general path on how to get there. So, our first step in creating our plan is to evaluate where we are now.

- Your height

- Your weight

- Your measurements

- Get lab work done. What are the numbers for your blood work? Keep them handy. Then after a couple of months of doing the right things, have that lab work redone. Compare and be encouraged by the improvements.

- Are you doing *any* exercise? Write down what you are presently doing—the type, number of minutes, reps, weight, stress level, speed—whatever is relevant so you can see how much you improve over time.

- Blood pressure. Does this number need to change? Are you currently taking medication (or need to) and want to use this number as motivation?

- Heart rate—resting and during exercise

- Body mass index (BMI) or percentage body fat. Yes, these might be horrifying numbers right now, but the point is to get you motivated now and encouraged later. If you're 40% fat, then at least you're 60% non-fat.

What other numbers or baselines are important to you or your doctor? Determine where you are now and set a general (or specific if you can) goal for what you want those baselines to be in the future. Then plan what you will do to get there.

God didn't scope out the earth and say, "Let there be all this good stuff right now." He took things one step at a time, one "day" at a time, one type of action at a time. He planned the work and then worked the plan. And that's what we need to do.

If your goal is physical fitness, how will you measure that? If through exercise, what type of exercise will it be? Think about what you will do, how long it'll take you at each exercise level, and how much of what kind of exercise you intend to be doing when you reach your goal and maintain it.

If your goal is weight loss, how will you achieve that? Do you have particular food dislikes or cravings you need to address? Has your doctor restricted your diet in any specific way? Does your diet need to be non-fat; low carb; vegetarian? What number of calories will you limit your eating to?

When it comes to dieting, I like to keep Proverbs 20:18 in mind.

> *Make plans by seeking advice; if you wage war, obtain guidance.*

Yes, weight loss is war. Ever hear of the "battle of the bulge"? You know as well as I do, that any pounds lost are because you've won the battle. So, it is critical to obtain guidance from those who know what they're doing; those who understand the miracle of our bodies created by God, and who have your best interests in mind. This includes doctors, nutritionists, dietitians; books; respectable Internet sites; weight loss counselors. You know the experts you need to seek guidance from for other health issues.

When you have a plan, you give yourself fewer opportunities to fail.

Write out your plan. God had a celestial white board to write His plan on. We have sheets of paper we can post right there in a place of honor on the front of our fridge! Write out your plan so you don't forget (or pretend to forget). Post it for the world to see. If you struggle keeping yourself in line, know that there are lots of other people willing to nag you to keep you on plan. Give them the plan so they can nag you well.

Then follow your plan. Review your plan weekly. Are you making progress? What parts of the plan are hardest or are not working? How do you need to change your plan? What might you try doing to make the plan work better? What have you learned about yourself and your plan over the past week? How can you use what you've learned for the better?

Most especially ask for accountability and encouragement from the Holy Spirit. He is already hovering over (and inside) your formless self; ready to mold and shape you.

Finally, if you have failed on your plan one day; begin again the next. Each beginning may be a small beginning. Remember that the Lord is rejoicing.

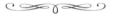

THINKING IT THROUGH: Are you a planner or do you like to fly by the seat of your big girl panties? Either way can work. For some of us, the more detailed our plan, the clearer our road and the less detours we'll make. For others, a general direction is all they need. Either way though you need to start out with knowing where you are and where you want to end up. And if you write those things down, you'll have a better chance of seeing your progress and being encouraged as you reach your destinations.

PRAYER: Heavenly Father, thank you for your perfect plan and for including me in it, most especially your plan of salvation. Thank you, Jesus for fulfilling that plan when there's nothing I could ever do to obtain salvation on my own. Holy Spirit help me create and follow a godly plan of reconstruction, knowing you are rejoicing even in my small beginnings. Amen.

SMALL BEGINNINGS
What simple plan can you create that will be easy to follow, yet detailed enough to know where you are headed?

Chapter 24

Let the Work Begin

O LORD our God, as for all this abundance that we have provided for building you a temple for your Holy Name, it comes from your hand, and all of it belongs to you (1 Chronicles 29: 16).

As Christians, we belong to God—body and soul. We gave Him our souls, of our free will. Our bodies and everything else in this universe, however, already belonged to God. He made us and we are His. Always have been. Always will be.

Throughout this book we have focused on being obedient to God in learning how we deal with our bodies. Maybe we made a few mistakes; took some steps forward; maybe a few temporary steps backward. Hopefully the forward steps brought us farther forward than the tripping tiptoes backwards.

Now as we look ahead, we consider the underlying point of everything in regard to rebuilding our temple. We belong to God. Until now, our emphasis has been we, us, our, I, me, my. Yes, we've tried to look at our bodies in relationship to God and His plan for us. But it has still been about *us*. By working to regain health and vitality, how will it benefit *us* so that *we* can live for Him?

The point we have not yet fully addressed is that we are not our own. These bodies belong to God. Before *we gave* ourselves to Jesus, these bodies were already His. We have never been more than caretakers of them.

We only get to use these bodies for a while. And while we are using them, we need to take good care of them. Otherwise, God will figure we're not good stewards of His possessions and may take them away from us before we're quite through! Yes, we'd end up in Glory but let's not rush things.

Remember also that we work for the Lord.

> *"Whatever you do, work at it with all your heart, as working for the Lord, not for men* (or yourselves)*"* (Colossians 3:23, explanation added).

That means God is the boss and it is time for our employee review.

Our bodies are the temple of the Lord. When Jesus took human form, His body was a temple, too. When He died, He raised his body temple again in three days because He was God. Rebuilding our temples will take a little longer. Months; perhaps years. Maybe even 46 years, like it took the Jews to rebuild the temple in Jerusalem.

We can make small beginnings each day, so that over time what we do is accumulatively better than where we began. God's temple in Jerusalem was built and rebuilt block by block with small beginnings. We can rebuild ours the same way.

These bodies are not our own, but they are ours to take care of. It is our job to recognize this trust and seek guidance from the Holy Spirit about how to improve on whatever good health we still have.

This book is about encouraging you to take small steps. If your goal is being more active and you started at zero, maybe now you've been able to just reduce the number of hours a day you sit. The next step will be to focus on being up and moving.

Then the focus might be on adding active things into your day, like gardening, vacuuming, stretching as you dust ceiling corners, parking farther from the store. Once you are comfortable with being more active you can focus on moving purposefully (as in some sort of structured exercise). But maybe that structured exercise at first is just to walk to the corner and back.

Most of all, this book is about living a spirit-filled life. My hope is that you will praise God and thank Him for whatever health you have and seek His guidance, through prayer, Scripture, fellowship with other godly women, and seeking the leading of the Holy Spirit, to rebuild these temples that belong to the Father, are saved by the Son, and are indwelt by the Holy Spirit.

Remember the verse we began with in Chapter 1:

> *Do not despise these small beginnings, for the LORD rejoices to see the work begin* (Zechariah 4:10 NLT).

Do not let a feeling of the enormous task in front of you overwhelm you. The Jewish people returned from exile to find the temple of the Lord demolished; the building blocks broken into rubble. The task before them was enormous. But they began the work. And the Lord rejoiced.

Know that every small beginning you take in rebuilding the temple where the Lord resides in you will result in the Lord rejoicing. Keep making small beginnings each day. Rejoice with the Lord!

With that thought in mind, here is one last verse of Scripture—this time from Nehemiah, the Governor in Jerusalem during the time the temple was being rebuilt. He urged the people of Jerusalem to pledge the following. We can do the same with these physical bodies where the Holy Spirit resides.

> *We promise together not to neglect the Temple of our God* (Nehemiah 10:39).

We begin the work. We continue the work. We do not neglect the Temple of our God. We—the Holy Spirit and I.

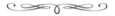

THINKING IT THROUGH: Reassess the progress you have made during this process, one focus point at a time. Do you need to focus more attention on any one area? What could your next step be for each area of your health?

PRAYER: Heavenly Father, thank you for my life and the health you have blessed me with. Thank you, Jesus for walking along side me during this journey and for holding me steady when I stumble. Holy Spirit renew my determination to create the strongest, most glorious temple I can for your holy presence. I ask these things in Jesus' precious and wonderful name. Amen.

SMALL BEGINNINGS
Assess the progress and commitments you have
made while reading this book. What has worked?
What do you need to revise? What is the next
small step you will take in your rebuilding
process, knowing the Lord is rejoicing?

Author's Thanks

Thank you for purchasing and reading this book! If you found this book helpful, I invite you to go Amazon.com and leave a review.

- Go to: www.Amazon.com

- Search for *Rebuild Your Tattered Temple*

- Click on this book title to bring up the book

- Then click on "leave a review"

You can find me online at CarolPetersonAuthor.com. I hope to see you there!

About the Author

Carol Peterson has been writing for publication for over 20 years. She writes to inspire, educate, and entertain. Her focus is sharing God's love with the world through a study of Scripture and opening other's eyes to see evidence of Jesus in the world around them.

She also writes books for children to help them understand this awesome and beautiful world.

You can find Carol Peterson online at her website CarolPetersonAuthor.com.

Books by Carol Peterson

From Honor Bound Books

With Faith Like Hers Bible Study Series: Studies on the character and circumstances of women in Scripture. Books available or coming soon:

- *I am Eve*
- *I am Esther*
- *I am Ruth*
- *I am Mary*
- *I am Elizabeth*
- *I am Rahab*
- *I am Hannah*
- *I am Deborah*

Flowers, Gemstones & Jesus: Finding Jesus in the Months of the Year

Rebuild Your Tattered Temple: Small Beginnings toward Better Health

Writer's Book Shelf Series

- *The Praying Writer: Prayers & Scripture for the Writing Process*
- *The Write Brand: Becoming Known in the World*
- *Working Together; Achieving Success: Critiquing, Marketing, Masterminds*
- *Writers as Entrepreneurs: It's Your Business*

Mustard Seed Books
(Children's Imprint of Honor Bound Books)
Books available or coming soon:

- *Counting Blessings* (Picture Book)
- *You and Me at the Sea* (Picture Book)
- *Baby Bliss* (Picture Book)
- *Stealing Sunlight: Bernie of Belleterre Book 1* (Middle Grade Novel)
- *Hydro Phobia: Bernie of Belleterre Book 2* (Middle Grade Novel)

From Libraries Unlimited

- *Fun with Finance: Math + Literacy = $uccess*
- *Jump into Science: Themed Science Fairs*
- *Around the World Through Holidays: Cross-Curricular Readers Theatre*
- *Jump Back in Time: A Living History Resource*

Resources

The best resource for every aspect of life, of course is the Holy Bible. I have quoted the New International Version throughout this book, reading Scripture in other versions during preparation, for inspiration and clarity.

There are a myriad of books and websites on every aspect of health available to you. Your first resource, however, should always be your personal physician.

To do additional research, head online and locate websites related to your particular health issue. Make sure the site, however, *is reputable* and well respected within the health care industry.

Here are a few of the websites I have relied on throughout the research and preparation of this book.

Cooper Institute www.cooperaerobics.com. Dr. Kenneth Cooper was the physician who headed the groundbreaking research on our body's need for cardiovascular exercise. In fact, Dr. Cooper was the man who coined the term *aerobics* to refer to type of exercise that worked the heart and lungs for minimum health. Any of his books are a great place to start when looking at exercise.

With the near epidemic of diabetes in America, the risk is there for many of us. A great place to begin to learn about controlling diabetes is the American Diabetes Association with the simple-to-remember web address of www.diabetes.org.

Dieting or thinking about it? One great place to begin to understand basic nutrition and calories in foods is CalorieKing.com.

If you are fighting or recovering from an illness, your doctor will be able to let you know about specific resources and/or recommended websites that may help you understand your particular illness and ways to help your body heal or fight against it.

My suggestion when you find a resource that is helpful to you, is to share it freely with a friend who might be suffering in the same way you are. Lift each other up. As Governor Nehemiah said, *"promise together not to neglect the Temple of our God"* (Nehemiah 10:39).

Made in the USA
Columbia, SC
25 September 2024

42396876R00100